Nicolas Cage

Hollywood's Wild Talent

Plexus, London

Published by Plexus Publishing Limited
55a Clapham Common Southside
London SW4 9BX
First Printing 1998

British Library Cataloguing in Publication Data

Robb, Brian J.
    Nicolas Cage : Hollywood's wild talent
    1. Cage, Nicolas 2. Motion picture actors and
    actresses - United States - Biography
    I. Title
    791.4'3'028'092

    ISBN 0 85965 264 5

Cover and book design by Mitchell Associates
Printed in Great Britain by
Hillman Printers (Frome) Ltd

10 9 8 7 6 5 4 3 2 1

Acknowledgements
Thanks are due to all the publications that have
covered the rise of Nicolas Cage over the years,
but the following were particularly of use:
Premiere (US edition), September 1990, 'Wild At
Heart' by Ralph Rugoff; Empire, September 1990,
'Wild At Heart' by Richard B. Woodward; Empire,
November 1990, 'Wings Of The Apache' by
Bridget Byrne; Empire, December 1990, 'Young
Nic' by Angie Errigo; Premiere (US Edition), May
1991, 'Last Tango In New Orleans' by Phoebe
Hoban; Empire, March 1993, 'Warning: Normality
Alert' by Jenny Cooney; Premiere (US edition),
December 1994, 'Made for TV Noir' by J.
Hoberman; Sight & Sound, March 1995, 'Hard and
Fast' by Manohla Dargis; Sight & Sound, June 1995,
'Method and Madness' by Manohla Dargis;
Premiere (UK edition), July 1995, 'Cherry Bomb:
Patricia Arquette' by Chris Heath; Sight & Sound,
February 1996, 'Things are Moving Very Quickly'
by Mike Figgis; Premiere (UK edition), February
1996, 'King of Pain' by Ryan Gibley; Neon, June
1997, 'The Accidental Hero' by Rob Tannenbaum;
Premiere, June 1997, 'Hollywood's Dark Prince' by
Larissa MacFarquhar; Neon, November 1997
'Harlem Fights: The Making of the Cotton Club' by
John Patterson.

    The Face, Attitude, Times Magazine, Interview,
Film Review, Variety, Hollywood Reporter, The
Village Voice, Movieline, Time, Entertainment
Weekly, People Magazine, Time Out.

    Thanks are also due to the invaluable BFI
Library and Information Services, everyone at the
film production, distributors and publicists' offices,
and all at Plexus.

    Thanks to the following photographic agencies
and sources for supplying photographs: All Action;
All Action/Fotoblitz; All Action/Shooting Star/Theo
Kingma; All Action/Paul Smith; The British Film
Institute; Camera Press; Camera Press/Mark
Anderson; Camera Press/Hubert Boesl; Circle
Films; Gamma Liaison/The Frank Spooner Agency;
Hollywood Pictures; Lumiere Pictures; Magellan
Pictures; MGM; New Line Cinema; Nova
International Films; Orion; Paramount Pictures;
Polygram Filmed Entertainment; Propaganda
Films; Tristar; 20th Century Fox; Valley 9000.

    It has not been possible in all cases to trace the
copyright sources, and the publishers would be
glad to hear from any such unacknowledged copyright holders.

Contents

1. Joining the Family

FOLLOWING HIS BEST ACTOR OSCAR for *Leaving Las Vegas* in 1996, Nicolas Cage has found himself transformed from something of a movie industry joke to one of Hollywood's biggest stars. He followed his Oscar win not with a slew of art movies but with a hugely successful trio of action films – *The Rock, Con Air* and *Face/Off*. His new-found status was confirmed when he was the number one choice for the leading part in the stalled Warner Brothers blockbuster *Superman Lives*.

Cage went from being regarded as an offbeat, kooky, sometimes extreme, method actor of the eighties with a series of quirky roles behind him to a nineties action hero, able to hold his own opposite top talents like Sean Connery, John Malkovich and John Travolta. Yet, the Oscar had shown he was equally capable of handling the very different demands of the role of a suicidal alcoholic out to drink himself to death. In fact, after the award, it seemed scarcely possible that anyone but Cage could have successfully tackled that part; but at the time he had little to prove and even less to lose. Before the Oscar Cage had been almost a laughing stock in Hollywood. If there was a bizarre role or a strange character that called for a fearless actor, Nic Cage would be top of the list.

Cage's start in the business was playing a series of rebellious punk kids in movies like *Valley Girl, Rumble Fish, Racing With The Moon* and *The Cotton Club*, and from then on he has continually reinvented himself on and off screen. He hopped back and forth between slightly strange romantic leads, opposite Kathleen Turner and Cher in *Peggy Sue Got Married* and Oscar-winner *Moonstruck*, to playing a publisher who thinks he's a vampire in *Vampire's Kiss*, to throwing himself into the over-the-top sex romp *Zandalee*. He was dubbed by the *Los Angeles Times* 'The crown prince of the darker realms of absurdity'.

This very diversity – action hero in *Wings Of The Apache, film noir* fall guy in *Red Rock West*, Jimmy Stewart-style comic foil in *Honeymoon In Vegas* and *It Could Happen To You* – allowed Nic to sneak up on Hollywood. While he was slowly gaining acclaim and ever-increasing box office for these performances, he was learning the ropes, preparing for his big chance in *Leaving Las Vegas*. Without the twelve years he put in prior to his Oscar-winning role, it's unlikely the golden statuette would be decorating the mantelpiece above the central fireplace in his gothic Hollywood mansion, among the framed *Superman* comic-book covers he collects.

Early in his career, preparation became everything for Nic. It was important for him to know his characters, to feel like them, to live like them. After all, if he was to convince an audience of the truth of his performance, he first had to convince himself. The lure of the much derided 'method' approach – where actors think themselves into the personality of the character they are to play and take on his or her character traits – obviously had strong attractions for Nic. As with some of the other extremes in his life, he would take this too far, famously having two teeth surgically removed and wearing his facial bandages on and off the set for five weeks for his role in *Birdy* . He even more notoriously chowed down on a live cockroach for a controversial scene in *Vampire's Kiss*. There were other cases, too – like the strenuous physical preparation he undertook for the role of a champion Canadian rower in *The Boy In Blue* and using the break-up of his romance with *Young Guns* actress Jenny Wright to fuel his character's romantic longings in *Moonstruck*.

His life off screen has been as complicated and convoluted as any of the characters he's played in his films. He was born Nicolas Coppola, but, determined not to build his career on nepotism, he changed his name to distance himself from his uncle, Francis Ford Coppola, acclaimed director of *The Godfather* and *Apocalypse Now*. Inspired by his interest in comic-books, he adopted the surname of black superhero Luke Cage.

With a variety of romances behind him, including with actresses Jenny Wright, Christina Fulton (with whom he has a son, Weston) and model Kristen Zang, as well as alleged flings with Uma Thurman, Cher and his *Honeymoon In Vegas* co-star Sarah Jessica Parker, Nic finally married actress Patricia Arquette in 1995. He'd first met Arquette casually in 1987, seven years before their wedding, but he announced to her then that they'd be married. Part of the problem some of the women in Nic's life had with him was his sometimes extreme and unpredictable behaviour – much of it connected to his preparations for early movie roles. Early in his career, for example, to play effectively the parts of the young thugs he was often cast as, Nic thought it would be a good idea to role play that type of character off screen, too. Although this alienated him from a lot of people, it also got him involved with a group of lifelong friends, many of whom also went on to become successful actors, among them award-winners Sean Penn and Jim Carrey.

From facing heavy criticism for his offbeat performance in his first notable film *Peggy Sue Got Married,* to acclaim for his romances, comedies and action roles, Nicolas Cage has proved he's got the right stuff to be a superstar. However, his fame and fortune have surprised no one more than Nic himself. He'd spent years going his own way and he was most surprised when he found himself being accepted into the wider Hollywood community. 'For the first time in my life my tastes were in synch with other people's. How weird is that? When you get an Oscar you are being recognised by your peers,' he noted. 'That was important to me. It told me I wasn't crazy all these years when I picked the roles I did. The award encourages me to keep following my heart. I've always tried to do the unexpected.'

Cage claims his Italian ancestry may have been Mafia connected: 'We come from a long line of robbers and highwaymen.'

Nicolas Cage was an unlikely nineties action hero: 'I've always tried to do the unexpected.'

However feted Nicolas Cage found himself in the late nineties, he was never celebrated for pulling off his biggest trick – inventing himself. After all, Nicolas Cage doesn't really exist.

Born Nicolas Kim Coppola on 7 January 1964, Nic's family connections predetermined he would be involved in the film industry. He was joining an Italian-American family with a history and a future in the entertainment business. His great-grandfather Francesco Pennino had arrived in the United States from Naples in Italy in the early years of the twentieth century. Pennino eventually found a role for himself playing piano for opera star Enrico Caruso, laying the foundations for an entertainment dynasty.

Settling into the Italian community in Brooklyn, New York, Pennino wasted no time in making contacts. When not playing the piano and composing his own songs, he set out to exploit the growing market for entertainment among the Italian community. He organised the importation of films from his homeland to be screened in America. This led to an offer of employment from movie studio Paramount, but Pennino declined. 'He didn't want his children in Hollywood,' claimed his daughter Italia, the irony not lost on her.

It was to be music, rather than film, that would bring the Pennino family into contact with the Coppola clan. Nic's paternal grandfather Carmine Coppola was a New York native who won a prestigious scholarship to the Julliard Academy. There he met another student, Albert Pennino, Francesco's son, an enthusiastic young trumpeter. Invited back to the Pennino family home, Carmine met and was enchanted by Albert's sister Italia. 'My father gave us all piano lessons,' recalled Italia of her childhood. 'Music comes from both sides of the family.'

Graduating from Julliard, Carmine Coppola took up a position at the Radio City Music Hall orchestra, married Italia and became the proud father of August Coppola, Nic's father, in 1934. Shortly thereafter, the Coppola family relocated to Detroit, with Carmine becoming the first flautist with the Detroit Symphony Orchestra, working his way up to become an arranger and eventually assistant conductor. On 7 April 1939 Carmine's second son, Francis Ford, was born in Detroit, partially named after the sponsor of Carmine's favourite musical radio programme, the *Ford Sunday Evening Hour*.

An offer of a position with the NBC Symphony Orchestra meant a return to New York for the growing Coppola clan, where Carmine worked for over a decade under the legendary conductor and composer Arturo Toscanini. The year 1946 saw another addition to the clan, with a sister for August and Francis Ford, named Talia. She recalled a difficult childhood as the family fortunes changed during the fifties after Carmine left the NBC Symphony Orchestra. 'There was a decade when things were shit,' she remembered, frankly. 'I travelled on the road with my father when I was nine years old – that should have been the decade of my development, instead it got lost in concern for my father.' Carmine's health deteriorated as he grew depressed at the need to travel the country to find work as a conductor-for-hire. Francis Ford also recalled the difficult times in the now impoverished household. 'It was a major theme of my family. One minute we had a little bit of money, the next my father was saying we couldn't afford the mortgage. It was tempestuous.'

Cage's father, August, seems to have come out of this period better than his younger siblings. 'Augie', as he was called by the others, spent his time encouraging and teaching his younger brother and sister, opening their eyes to music, literature and theatre. 'He was a cultured man,' recalled Talia of her older brother. 'He was always very supportive, a natural teacher.'

Once his son had got to university Carmine hoped Augie would go on from a successful academic career to become a doctor. Instead, armed with a PhD in Comparative Literature, August went on to develop a revolutionary approach to teaching blind students. He invented the 'tactile dome', a sensory aid which allows blind people to experience their surroundings other than through sight, which is now on display in San Francisco's science museum, the Exploratorium. As August further developed his academic career, eventually becoming the Dean of Creative Arts at San Francisco University, his success was eclipsed by that of his younger brother, Francis Ford.

Throughout the sixties and seventies, Francis Ford Coppola was the true successor to Francesco Pennino and his forays into the world of show business. Graduating from UCLA film school, Coppola moved on from low-budget Roger Corman-produced thriller *Dementia 13* to directing the musical *Finian's Rainbow*, before hitting the big time with the personal film *The Rain People*. His real calling card, though, was the international blockbuster *The Godfather*, drawn from Mario Puzo's novel. Since then his career has been a roller coaster ride, from bankruptcy to artistic acclaim and back again several times.

August Coppola was sensitive to his brother's high-profile success and fame, even though August was the one to enjoy the more stable life and career. In 1960, just as his brother was embarking on a film directing career, August met and married young dance choreographer Joy Vogelsang. She was a creative but unpredictable talent who would cause August and their sons, including Nicolas, much concern in the years to come. Before Nicolas Coppola arrived on the scene, he was preceded by two older brothers – Marc, later a New York radio disc jockey, and Christopher, also to become a film director like his Uncle Francis.

Born into such a talented and wildly unpredictable family, Nicolas Cage was destined to work somewhere in the entertainment industry. It's something he realised from early in his life. A childhood spent in cinemas awaited him. August, and sometimes Uncle Francis, would take the Coppola kids to the local art cinema, rather than to see the latest Disney cartoon. Instead of the tales of *Snow White And The Seven Dwarfs* and *Bambi*, young Nicolas grew up watching Akira Kurosawa's samurai dramas and the work of silent film stars like 'man of a thousand faces' Lon Chaney, famous for changing his looks in thrilling horror classics like *The Hunchback Of Notre Dame*, *The Phantom Of The Opera* and *London After Midnight*. He was much impressed by German expressionist cinema, especially Fritz Lang's films like *Metropolis* and F. W. Murnau's 1922 'unofficial' version of Bram Stoker's *Dracula, Nosferatu* starring the skeletal Max Schreck.

It wasn't all movies for the young Coppolas. Family history would be related as the trio listened to scratchy recordings of their great-grandfather Francesco Pennino performing. But family life was not free of complications, and as his childhood developed, Nicolas Cage found real-life concerns impinging more and more on him. 'I always had to deal with things,' he recalled. 'It started with my mother.'

During the late sixties and into the early seventies August Coppola had much to cope with. His wife Joy, daughter of Louise Vogelsang, was unstable and suffered from a series of depressions and mental breakdowns which almost pulled the family apart. His mother's mental health problems and frequent institutionalisation are not subjects Nic has ever been comfortable talking about.

'She was a very gentle, sensitive woman,' he once remembered. 'If I look at home movies of when I was two years old, I see that she was a very caring mother, the way she touched me. For lengths of time she was naturally "out there", naturally surreal, with all kinds of poetry flying out of her. It gave me an original perspective.'

As August held down his university job at Cal State and tried to provide for his family, Joy was falling apart. Her periods of depression and dissatisfaction with life increased, even though she and the family were living a nice, middle-class kind of suburban existence in Hackett Avenue, Long Beach, in Los Angeles. Joy consulted doctors and counsellors to find a cure for her troubles, but from August's point of view her behaviour became more and more extreme and ever more unacceptable in a family environment. Once, during a heated argument about her condition and possible treatments, Joy claimed that Nicolas was not August's son. Joy told August of a supposed relationship with actor Robert Mitchum. Nicolas has always said that the outburst was a malicious lie aimed at hurting his father, but it seems to have had an effect on August, who later became hostile towards his son.

'The Mitchum business started when they were fighting and she wanted to get a rise out of him,' said Nic of his father's suspicions. 'She said to him, "Nicky's not your child." She had a signed photograph of Robert Mitchum which said: "To Joy, Love and Kisses, Bob" and she always made hints. Obviously, nothing happened. She was just a young lady in a dance group and Mitchum was around and she got an autographed picture. She admitted to me that she told him that in the heat of anger. I'm sure she doesn't feel good about it, but you know how people say things in the heat of anger. I've lived with that anger from my father for thirty years.'

Nic has no doubts whatsoever about his paternity. 'The fact is if you look at a picture of my dad and you look at me, it's obvious that I'm his son. There has always been an edge from my father towards me and that must be the reason. There was this "thing".'

As Joy's condition deteriorated, August took control, demanding she seek professional treatment. Nicolas Cage became aware of these troubles and they would lead to his parents divorce as he turned twelve. At first, he had to understand the reasons why his mother would leave home for long periods. 'She would go away for years at a time. When she got too erratic, she went . . . away. My childhood consisted of going to see her, going in there with the crazy people. She was institutionalised for years and went through shock treatments.'

The course of electro-therapy shocks that Joy Vogelsang underwent seemed to cure her condition for short periods of time, and she would return to the family home, only to vanish from young Nicolas's life again a few months later. 'The hardest part was going to visit her in the institutions,' recalled Cage. 'Sometimes she would go into Rip Van Winkle mode and forget everything that had happened. Even when things got really bizarre, I was able to detach and look at it with a scientific curiosity. I'm sure it had some impact on me, though. Maybe her illness was behind the nightmares I had. The hardest part was seeing someone I love suffer.'

Young Nicolas was plagued by nightmares as a child, from visions of scary clowns to giant female genies who would pester him when he was on the toilet. His mother's plight was often the subject of such nocturnal scarefests. 'I used to have nightmares that my mother's head was attached to a cockroach's body, and she was living in the garage. That really freaked me out, so I was really horrified of bugs.' It was to overcome this fear that Nicolas would later confront the bug-eating scene in his film *Vampire's Kiss* full on, and would also build up a bug collection during his early acting years.

August Coppola was having to cope with his family breakdown, just as his brother was enjoying his greatest success with the release of *The Godfather* in 1972. The fame and fortune bestowed on Francis Ford Coppola as a result of the movie allowed him to purchase a sprawling wine-producing ranch in the Napa Valley, north of San Francisco. This turn of events served to fuel August's jealousy and resentment of his younger brother's fame and success.

Young Nicolas watched as his father struggled, realising his suffering, but also in retrospect realising that his mother's illness had bestowed on him an invaluable series of experiences he later used in his acting career. 'His blood pressure went up and he did most of the raising of us,' said Nicolas of his father. 'It was really hard on him, but I wouldn't change it for anything, in one way. I think it made my life rich and gave me a depth of emotion. It's like a blessing in disguise. I gained something from it – it gave me an insight and a sensitivity that I don't think I would have had.'

Despite his family tribulations, young Nicolas did his best to enjoy as normal a childhood as he could, and his father certainly set out to make it easier for the children. 'He was always doing things to encourage our imaginations,' said Nic of August. 'I remember my father as being this Sean-Connery-as-James-Bond type. When he took me to see *Dr No* at the drive-in, I imagined myself as James Bond's son. I learned some of what being a man was about by watching James Bond. I loved that image. My father had this very professional air about him, but he always approached things with a great deal of creativity.' His Aunt Talia recalled the home life of the three young Coppolas: 'It was very natural that you were given reading lists.'

Although he had two brothers, Nicolas spent much of his childhood on his own, entertaining himself in a variety of imaginative ways which would feed into his bizarre life as an actor. 'I had a very active imagination and dream life,' he admitted. 'I was quite content playing by myself. When I was four my father took me to Italy, to the town where the author of *Pinocchio* was born. All they did there was sell Pinocchios – I still have one. The story parallels my life a bit – the whole "an actor's life for me" thing, being a puppet who loses his strings. One day I was upset about breaking my little Pinocchio toy, so my father planted its head in the garden and told me to water it. A couple of days later a giant wooden Pinocchio had grown in its place – my father had placed it there. After that, I started planting my Hot Wheels cars with the hope that one of them would blossom into a real car, but it never quite worked the same.'

Inspired by reading hundreds of comic-books and identifying with the characters in the brightly coloured, ink-smudged pages, six-year-old Nicolas would retreat 'into an imaginary world where I could go to and be all these other characters. I must've been in my own world, trying to get away from whatever crisis was happening at home. I had this ability to reinvent myself.'

It wasn't only in his imagination that Nicolas would reinvent himself. He loved dressing up and play-acting, stealing items from his mother's wardrobe, and from his grandparents. Disguises were a constant source of fascination. 'I thought the coolest thing you could do was dress yourself up as somebody else. I loved Hallowe'en and costumes. As a child in Long Beach I spent a lot of time pretending I was other people. I was into the whole concept of trying to disguise myself.' Nicolas thoroughly enjoyed an early seventies TV show called *Toma*, which starred Tony Musante as a detective who was also a dab hand at using disguises to solve his cases. 'I thought that was really cool,' said Nicolas.

Disguises also had a practical benefit for Nicolas as they helped him avoid bullies at school. In the fourth grade, he was the subject of attention for one particular nasty who would steal his Twinkies or beat him up. Putting his imagination to practical use, he dressed up in his older brother's clothes, slicked his hair back and confronted the bully on the school bus. 'I got some black Ray Ban sunglasses,' he said. 'I stuck some chewing gum in my mouth, got my older brother's cowboy boots, and had this swagger when I got on the bus.' Taking charge of the situation, Nicolas claimed to be Nicky Coppola's tough cousin. He told the bully that if he messed with Nicky one more time, he'd 'get his ass kicked'. His bravado worked and the bully backed off, leaving Nicolas to travel to school on the bus in peace. 'They bought it. They never beat up on me again. It was really my first experience with acting, with changing myself. I learned I could act, that there was power in being able to act.' It was Nicolas Cage's first great performance.

His interest in acting was sparked quite early as he would spend happy hours in front of the family's television, absorbed by the fantastic stories the box brought into his home. 'When I was six, I wanted to escape inside the TV. I wanted to get into the set as amazing things happened there – dinosaurs were inside the TV, and Jerry Lewis. I remember being on my living room floor on a red carpet and we had an oval-shaped, '65 Zenith set – I still have it, but no one can fix it. That was the reason I wanted to act, because I was so mystified by the tiny people.' He even applied to feature on the TV game show *The Dating Game*, aged only thirteen. 'My parents wouldn't let me be on it,' lamented Nicolas of his first attempt to break into television.

Apart from featuring in family home movies, Nicolas was also the star of his brother Christopher's home-made Super-8 film epics. 'The first role I ever had was as Superboy, in the back yard with my brother Chris,' said Nicolas, who would later be chosen to play Superman on the big screen. 'I was about twelve. I came from the kind of family that always wanted to create things.' According to his maternal grandmother Louise Vogelsang, the three Coppola kids would beaver away for hours creating 'little monster movies' in the backyard. This play-acting was to feed into their future professional lives. 'Nic was my leading man,' remembered Christopher, who was later to direct his brother professionally in the feature film *Deadfall*. 'He really put himself into these movies. He loved it, always loved it. He was a natural performer. There was nothing he didn't want to try and do.'

While the ambition to take up acting as a career was fermenting in his mind, young Nicolas was pursuing other, more daredevil possibilities. 'I thought I was Evel Knievel. I saw George Hamilton play him in the movie, and I remember thinking how cool he was, the way he would rev his bike, adjust his chain, wipe the grease off his boot – all in slow motion – then do the ultimate jump over twenty vans. That changed my life. From then on I started jumping over beer kegs with my bicycle. That wasn't enough, so I made a big hoop out of cardboard and doused it in kerosene. I announced to the whole neighbourhood that I was going to jump through this hoop of fire. Word quickly got out and all these kids started paying money to watch me do it – but when the big day came, my dad found out and shut the whole thing down.'

With a career as a daredevil unlikely, Nicolas had to concentrate on working hard at school while he considered his options. He attended a variety of elementary schools in the Los Angeles area, often being thrown out for his poor behaviour. 'I was expelled regularly from elementary school for being a prankster.' On one notable occasion he laced his classmates egg salad sandwiches with fried grasshoppers bought in a Chinatown store and sat back to watch them eat up the surprise fillings. 'I got caught and was expelled. I went to a very rough school.' Playing the clown at school was another way of escaping the troubles at home for Nicolas, but it was also a way of ensuring ever more trouble for himself. Academically he was doing well, with the potential to follow in his father's footsteps one day, but his endless game-playing spoilt his prospects. He didn't particularly like school and even thought of running away. 'Classes were always a bore to me. I wanted to learn things on my own, not by presentations. I was a loudmouth and a clown. It came as a surprise to me, later, that I could be serious and still get attention. At one point in my early teens I was pretty certain that I was going to join the merchant marines and get on a boat and do the Melville thing,' he recalled with humour.

During his adolescence, Nicolas became fascinated by movie stars, aware that his Uncle Francis was making a living by telling them what to do in blockbuster movies. In a precursor of things to come much later in the movie *Face/Off*, he spent much of the mid-seventies trying to look like John Travolta, who was enjoying success in the TV series *Welcome Back Kotter*, before hitting the big time with *Saturday Night Fever*. Each movie he saw would instil in Nicolas a desire to be like the character on screen or to become like the actor playing the leading part. 'I saw a Bruce Lee movie and wanted to be him very badly, so started working out when I was twelve. I used to do all these sit-ups in the morning, then go to school as well. I studied Kung Fu, too.' Acting was never far from his mind. 'I'd walk around school, acting out the characters in whatever I was reading. When I read Kafka's *Metamorphosis* I was a cockroach for a week.'

After years of trying to hold things together, Nicolas's father August finally gave up and divorced his mother, Joy. It was a sad time for the twelve-year-old Nicolas, but it also resolved some issues which had been causing tension in the household. 'It was a sad day, but it was a good day,' claimed Nicolas, recalling his parent's official break-up. 'I remember my mother wanting to have custody and I knew she loved us. It wasn't traumatic – I was relieved. It was uncomfortable, though. I had to sit down and talk with the judge. I smiled the whole way through the meeting. I was sad about the custody because my mother obviously wasn't able to raise us, yet she still tried to be strong and have dignity.'

His years of watching TV shows portraying the perfect family life had not prepared Nicolas for this day. 'You see shows like the *Brady Bunch* and they paint pictures of a family without problems. That's not fair – it makes everybody feel like they are abnormal. My mother's fine now and very jolly with a terrific sense of humour, but much time was lost. She's always had a wonderful imagination and been a huge influence in my work because she was just naturally kind of surreal.'

Following the divorce the Coppola family relocated, with August moving them to the outskirts of Beverly Hills, hoping to take advantage of the area's superior school system and give Nicolas the chance he deserved to get a good education.

August found a house on La Cinega Boulevard and Hamilton Drive, just on the edge of Los Angeles's most affluent district. As a result, Nicolas found himself attending Beverly Hills High School, which probably boasts some of the richest school pupils in the whole of the United States and was featured in the Fox teen soap *Beverly Hills 90210*. 'I didn't like high school. I was a nerd and didn't fit in,' admitted Nicolas, feeling out of place as his family was not as well off as those of his classmates, despite the fact that his uncle was now a world famous and mega-rich film director. 'I hate saying I went to Beverly Hills High because it suggests that I came from a rich family. The truth is that my father was supporting three kids on a teacher's salary. Going to a school like Beverly Hills High where all the kids have money, and they're driving to school in Porsches and Ferraris and I'm taking the bus, was frustrating to say the least. I couldn't ask a girl out because I'd have to ask her to take the bus with me. We didn't have a lot of money, but people would say to me: "But you're Francis Ford Coppola's nephew, why don't you drive a sports car?"'

His situation did not escape the attention of his teachers, either. Nicolas's former music teacher at Beverly Hills High School Joel Pressman recalls the student feeling out of place because affording things for school didn't come as easily to his family as it did to some others. 'I remember he had trouble paying for a pair of dress shoes to wear with his madrigal singers' costume,' recalled Pressman.

Since the fifties, the status symbol for all American high schoolers was the cool car. It was not only a form of transport, but a handy venue away from parents to indulge in necking sessions. In fact, Nicolas's Uncle Francis had produced George Lucas's film *American Graffiti*, which dealt exactly with that topic, with the action set in the pre-Vietnam war era. For Nicolas, though, his troubles were not over, even when he did have a car. 'I got my first Triumph Spitfire when I was sixteen and my father wouldn't let me drive it,' he said, recalling another source of friction between him and August. 'I would sit in the car and pretend to drive it. In the meantime, he would drive it. I bought it with my own money, but I had to watch him drive it with the top down . . .'

Due to his car troubles, Nicolas's Prom Night was almost a disaster. Even after registering the car and gaining his licence, he discovered to his horror that it continually broke down. He took his frustrations out on the vehicle when it did go. His school friend Tony Darren remembered some hairy incidents riding around town with him. 'He would floor it, and he'd run into trash cans and have them flying off the roof,' claims Darren. 'Just anything to create some kind of havoc.'

Cashing in savings bonds given to him and his brothers by their grandmother, Louise Vogelsang, Nicolas rented a tuxedo and a limo for his Prom date. Nonetheless, the evening still took a distinctly weird turn, with Nicolas's fear of his date overwhelming him. 'We're at the Prom and I kissed her,' remembered Nicolas. 'When she responded, I was so nervous I started throwing up. The limo driver wouldn't let me back in the car because there was vomit on my shoes. So I walked home. That was my Prom.'

Nicolas had first got interested in girls while watching TV and had a list of fantasy women who caught his attention. Catwoman in the colourful *Batman* TV series was a favourite, 'because of the suit, but I don't think there was anybody who looked

Nic's uncle, Francis Ford Coppola, on the set of The Godfather *in Sicily.*

better in black leather than Mrs Peel in *The Avengers*. I was amazed by that.'

Nicolas had been banned by his father from seeing his uncle's film *The Godfather* when it came out in 1972 and August had cruelly made his son throw out a bunch of promotional T-shirts that Francis Ford Coppola had delivered, but it was that film which gave the teenage Nicolas his first sexual thrill. 'There was that scene where Al Pacino kisses that beautiful Sicilian woman and she takes her bra off. I remember I was feeling new things. It really turned me on.'

He was also a big fan of the TV series *I Dream Of Jeannie*, and blames the view of women he got from Barbara Eden's role as 'causing me a great deal of difficulty in my life. When you follow the Jeannie course, you're in trouble. There are women who know how to play the genie role, and use it as a net – the perfect woman who will do anything for you and make magical things happen. Then they catch you, and you're the one that's stuck inside the bottle.' In later life, Nicolas would be reluctant to commit to relationships.

As if being taunted at school for not sharing in the wealth of his Uncle Francis was not enough, Nicolas was given a short-lived taste of that opulence when he was sent to live for a short time on his uncle's ranch in the Napa Valley. With his older brothers having moved away from home, Nicolas's father August planned a summer lecture tour of America, taking a break from his current teaching post at Cal State in Long Beach, and Nicolas couldn't come along. Nicolas found himself entering his uncle's domain stewing in jealousy. 'I was in this wonderful house with wonderfully generous people, but it wasn't my stuff, it wasn't my house. I felt like "Why is it that they have all this stuff and my brothers and I don't? I want to get some of that . . ."'

16

Feeling the outsider in the family, Nicolas found his ambitions taking shape the longer he stayed, ambitions which had the potential to bring him some of the riches enjoyed by one side of his family, but not by him, his brothers and his father. 'I vowed then that I would go to Los Angeles, learn to act and then one day buy my own Victorian mansion in San Francisco. It was unfortunate that it was revenge which fuelled my ambition.'

Knowing his father would not approve of his real plans, upon his return to Los Angeles Nic announced he wanted to be a writer. It was his way of attending the drama department of Beverly Hills High without stirring things up at home. 'I always said that's what I wanted to be to impress him, but I wasn't being honest with myself,' he admitted. 'Now, whenever I do write and finish a story or do a painting, I feel very satisfied because I know I've done it for all the right reasons.' Nic knew that his father's jealousy of Francis would mean that he could never approve of his son wanting to pursue a career in Hollywood. Encouraged by his father to write, Nicolas was in fact auditioning for roles in plays and taking acting lessons. When one audition resulted in him being late returning home, his secret was out. His aunt, Talia Shire, reckons Nic 'got up and blew the class away' during the audition. His father, however, exploded with rage: 'You're never going to become an actor, Nicolas! Why don't you just forget it.' All the tensions and resentments which had built up between the two – from August's fear about his son's paternity to Nicolas's questions about his father's responsibility for his mother's illnesses – spilled out that evening. It was a turning point in their relationship, one from which the pair would never fully recover. Nowadays Nic is philosophical about what was said, taking from his father's rage and his uncle's success what he needed to provide him with the motivation to become an actor. 'Later he said he did it to make me want to prove him wrong,' said Nicolas of his father's outburst, 'but I don't believe him. There was always this strange dynamic with my father. He's given me so much in terms of my ability to look at the world, but at the same time there's this "thing" . . .'

Whatever the motives for the argument, Nicolas had made up his mind. 'There was a certain resolve,' recalled his eldest brother Marc of Nicolas's decision to pursue acting seriously. 'With Nic you knew that his determination would get him what he wanted.' But while he wanted the wealth and fame that Francis enjoyed, he also learned lessons from his uncle's periodic failures. 'I've had a strange relationship with money,' he noted, 'because I've seen it from an early age and I've seen its powerful effects.'

It was clear to Nicolas that the easiest way to succeed in Hollywood would be to trade on the family name, to make use of being a Coppola, to emphasise his links to the acclaimed director of the *Godfather* films. It was tempting, but it was not in his nature. He was not above pumping his uncle for useful industry information and acting hints and tips, but Nic was too individualistic and too proud of his own abilities to rely on nepotism.

2. Grudges and Passions

HAVING A FILM DIRECTOR UNCLE didn't make it as easy as he hoped for Nicolas Cage to break into the industry. 'I don't think people were equipped to take me seriously as an actor,' Nic recalled of his early efforts, under the Coppola name. 'It made me work twice as hard.'

Despite the tensions and squabbles, envy and fall outs among the Coppola clan, Nicolas Cage knows that he owes his determination to succeed to his ancestry. 'It's a family that's loaded with grudges and passions,' he told *Playboy* magazine. 'We come from a long line of robbers and highwaymen in Italy, you know. Killers, even.'

The killer instinct was something the young would-be actor would have to work at developing. For the time being, he was driven by aspiration. He wanted the kind of success he'd seen at his Uncle Francis's ranch in the Napa Valley – the money, the house, the security that came from wealth. And he figured acting was his best bet to achieve that, not teaching or in academia as his father had always dreamed.

The relationship between August and Nicolas was fraught during his teens, and it continues to be so today. It fed into the films he enjoyed watching; Nicolas would claim his favourite movie was *East Of Eden*, the 1955 Elia Kazan film starring James Dean. The central father-son relationship in the film captured his imagination. In fact, Dean became something of a role model for him. 'The scene where he gives the money to his father and his father refuses to take it, and he cries . . . that's when I knew I wanted to be an actor, like him,' he said. James Dean's rebel figure was to heavily influence his approach to his early acting roles, leavened with a dash of the young Marlon Brando.

First, though, he had to expand his acting experience beyond the drama department of Beverly Hills High. He was highly active in the theatre group and according to his music teacher Joel Pressman he 'became the focal point of every scene'. When he was surprisingly passed over for a featured part in the student production of *West Side Story*, Nic felt he'd gained all the benefit he could from the school. It was time to move on, and as he was in his senior year, he'd be due to leave soon anyway. He sat and passed his General Educational Development test and left the school as soon as he could.

San Francisco was to be his destination, where he enrolled for a summer course with the American Conservatory Theatre. He was only fifteen, but was determined to succeed in this new environment. Shortly after his arrival he was cast in a stage production of Clifford Odets' *Golden Boy*, a tale of trial in the boxing ring. It was a great experience and made the young man feel like a 'real' actor at last. 'He believed he could do it,' claimed his brother Marc. 'That's the great gift he has – he believed in himself.'

Television was the next lure for Nicolas – he wanted to be on the flickering tube that had so captured his imagination when growing up. He'd been seen in a student production of *Oklahoma* while at Beverly Hills High by Hollywood personal manager Chris Viores. He contacted Nicolas and encouraged him to begin auditioning for parts on TV series. It was to be film roles that would ultimately attract Nic, but a stepping stone part on a TV show could do no harm, he figured, as long as it was a short-term thing. He soon won a role, as a pumped-up surfer on the TV series pilot movie *The Best Of Times*, a beach-set teen soap that pre-dated *Baywatch* by a decade. 'I was seventeen when I got the part. It was a very bad television show, but just me getting the part surprised everyone, because I'd kept what I was up to to myself. It wasn't very good, but I still feel proud about it because it was something that happened of its own accord. It did the job – the family gradually warmed up to me being an actor.'

While August was never going to wholeheartedly endorse his son's choice of career, Uncle Francis was much more positive. But however much he thought his family connections might get him work, the then Nicolas Coppola found the name was actually a barrier at film auditions. 'Casting agents would spend the entire audition asking about my uncle Francis,' he told *Entertainment Weekly*. 'Directors and casting agents didn't want to know me because of my surname. They used to say, "Well, this guy's connected – we don't want to give him a shot."' The frustration planted an idea in Nicolas's head. If he were to change his name he might win parts and succeed in spite of being a Coppola. Before he took such a drastic step, though, he had a big audition coming up.

Up for the co-starring role of Brad in Amy Heckerling's film *Fast Times At Ridgemont High*, he attended the audition under the name Nicolas Coppola. It was 1982 and Nicolas was seventeen – just the right age to play in the ensemble 'brat pack' film about good times at high school. The film was based on a book by Cameron Crowe, who was later to have success with his own films *Singles* and *Jerry Maguire*. The leading actor was Sean Penn, playing a spaced-out surfer dude. It wasn't to be, however. Nicolas lost out on the part of Brad to Judge Reinhold (later Cage's co-star in *Zandalee*) for whom it turned out that the film was a springboard to a career as a comic foil for Eddie Murphy in the *Beverly Hills Cop* movies. While he fumed that his name may have lost him the part, Nicolas was pleased to be hired anyway for the far less significant role of 'Brad's buddy'. At least it was a film role, even if much of what he did shoot ended up being snipped out of the film and he was listed way down the credits, coming in 21st on the cast listing.

Fast Times At Ridgemont High was to be a learning experience – and it was to be the last time he'd use his real name in a film audition which didn't involve his Uncle Francis. Sean Penn proved to be an inspiration for Nicolas – and the pair quickly became firm friends and drinking buddies. 'I would watch Sean and get ideas,' said Nic of his time on the film. 'He was so good and confident.'

Even among his fellow cast members – all young up-and-coming talents like him, including Jennifer Jason Leigh, Phoebe Cates, Eric Stoltz, *ER*'s Anthony Edwards and James Russo – Nicolas Coppola was something of a joke. They seemed to think he was merely slumming it on the film, waiting for his uncle to step in and make him a star, while they had to win roles mostly without any movie industry connections. 'I was the brunt of jokes because my name was still Coppola. They said I was there because of Francis. I felt the burden of being his nephew,' Nic noted. 'On the set, some of the actors would get together outside my trailer and recite a version of Robert Duvall's line from *Apocalypse Now.*'

Duvall's famous line was 'I love the smell of napalm in the morning,' altered by the cast hassling Nicolas to: 'I love the smell of Nicolas in the morning.' 'It was psychologically hard,' admitted the neophyte actor. 'No matter how good you feel you are, you are not good enough. I really had something to prove to the others. I felt I had to work twice as hard as the next guy to prove myself.'

Instead of being the key to success he hoped, the Coppola name was turning out to be a burden. Those vague thoughts of doing something about it became more concrete in Nicolas's mind, but first intervention from his uncle would provide him with some further valuable acting experience. 'Being a Coppola is a mixed blessing,' said Nicolas. 'Francis is a powerful man who enjoys his position.'

The problem with Francis Ford Coppola's position is that it has been incredibly variable. While Nicolas was growing up and into his teens, his uncle was on a roll, from *The Godfather* through *The Conversation* to *The Godfather Part Two.* Francis Ford Coppola was directing, his sister Talia Shire was acting in his films and his father Carmine was composing music for the movies, which led to an Oscar in 1975. It was a family business. However, Francis was a maverick, single-minded and stubborn. Like his contemporaries, George Lucas and Steven Spielberg, Coppola was determined to do things his own way. Founding his own studio – American Zoetrope – he set out to make a big-budget hit, but his *One From The Heart*, featuring Frederic Forrest, Nastassja Kinski and Teri Garr was a glorious flop, bringing down the studio and Francis Ford Coppola with it in 1982.

The only way out of the financial mess was to work, to make movies and so generate income. Coppola had secured the rights to two S. E. Hinton books – *The Outsiders* and *Rumble Fish* – both tales of teenage rebellion. He set out to make a couple of quick low-budget movies featuring as much young talent as he could round up. The result was a call to his nephew Nicolas asking him to audition.

'I auditioned for him for the role of Dallas in *The Outsiders*,' remembered Nicolas. 'I was there for nine hours, but I was so nervous I didn't know what I was doing.' In preparation for the part he locked himself in a room for two weeks, drinking beer and staring at a picture of Charles Bronson, hoping somehow that the physical and mental attitude to play a hooligan would rub off on him. It was a first tentative foray into the realms of method acting that would later come to dominate the first half of his Hollywood career. His efforts were, however, all in vain.

After he had waited for hour after nervous hour, Francis announced he wanted Nicolas to try out for the part of Two-Bit instead of Dallas. The change of role threw Nicolas totally, and some of the resentment he had been feeling towards Francis Ford Coppola for the problems he'd been having at auditions due to sharing the same name came out in a fumbling, angry and incompetent performance. Nicolas knew he was doomed. 'I couldn't change gear and everything fell apart,' he said ruefully. 'I was in hospital for a while after that and decided I didn't want to act anymore.' Matt Dillon played Dallas and Emilio Estevez, brother of Charlie Sheen, took the role of Two-Bit. Nicolas Coppola went off to lick his wounds, recovering from his stress-induced illness and resolving to give up on the acting business altogether.

He was now damned three times. His father didn't want him to act and it was causing problems in the family, his family name prevented him from acting as he lost role after role, and now his film director uncle didn't want to give him a part either. He just couldn't win. It was the final straw. 'I had just auditioned for *The Outsiders*, and I'd reached the point in the Hollywood rejection system most actors go through where I got pretty down on myself,' he recalled. 'So I thought, well, I'll try this one more time, but if it doesn't work, I'm going to get on a boat and write.' Reconsidering his rash decision to give up acting, and tiring of the job he had taken selling popcorn at the Fairfax Theatre (it was as close to a movie career as he thought he might get), Nicolas decided instead to rise to the challenge, to reinvent himself and to pull off the greatest acting part of all. He'd change his name and play the part of a rising young actor in real life.

The decision had been a long time coming, and to help him choose a new identity, Nicolas went to visit his maternal grandmother Louise Vogelsang, who was known affectionately as Divi. Sitting at her kitchen table, the pair ran through variations on his name, hoping to find something that worked as a Hollywood identity. It was like the old studio days when studio heads would routinely change the names of actors and actresses to make them less ethnic or more 'Hollywood'. Their first choice was Nicolas Vogel, but they decided it was not streamlined enough. Next up was Nicolas's favourite colour, Blue, as a possible surname. It was short and snappy, easy to remember and catchy, but somehow seemed too fake.

Nicolas was worried about losing his Italian heritage in the name change and suggested Mascalzone, Italian for 'bad boy', a reference to his James Dean influences. It was too long and too foreign for Hollywood. Jokingly, Nicolas came up with Nicolas Faust as he was, after all, selling his soul to the movie industry in a desperate attempt to escape the cage he found himself in. Then they had it – Cage, Nicolas Cage. It was the name of his favourite comic strip character, the black superhero Luke Cage, and the name of a composer admired by his father, John Cage – an ideal way of placating everyone concerned about his change of name. 'I'd always loved the name Cage because of Luke Cage, Power Man,' he said, seeing it as symbolic of his desire for escape and change. 'It was a matter of freedom.'

At the time, Nic claimed he faced a lot of hostility from Coppola relatives for his decision. 'My great-great-great-grandfather came to America from Italy and, you know, we were paupers struggling, and then my grandfather Carmine developed a talent, which was to play the flute. Carmine married my grandmother, who was a songwriter's daughter, and that began this sort of illustrious life in the arts. With that is a certain kind of competition and pride and a thick kind of passion that I guess by changing my name I ended. The family was pissed off because I changed my name.'

However, as soon as he heard of the name change, Francis Ford Coppola sent his nephew a telegram of congratulations, and signed it 'Francis Cage'. 'Nicolas had his own identity,' believed Francis Ford Coppola of his nephew. 'He wanted to accentuate that. My thought then, as now, is that he is a Coppola and we are proud of him and wish his name was still Coppola.' August kept silent, rarely contacting his son at all since he'd left home. It was a tough decision, but one that Nic felt he had to take. He buried his previous persona and set out anew to face the harrowing world of auditions as Nicolas Cage. 'When I first started going to auditions and using my own name, it was obvious that everyone was thinking of twenty years of someone else's history. There is a kind of fear that comes with nepotism. Directors have their own egos – they didn't want to hire someone named Coppola to be in their picture. His name was too "big". As Nic Cage, the first audition I did was the best one I'd ever had. That told me I'd done the right thing.'

Desperate as he was to escape the Coppola name, Nicolas Cage found himself drawn back into the family fold when Francis Ford Coppola called him and asked him to help out in auditioning other actors for roles in his film of S. E. Hinton's *Rumble Fish*. Nic's job was to read scenes with actors trying out for parts in the movie. He wasn't auditioning for a role himself, but he saw it as a good opportunity to flex his acting muscles in an audition scenario where the pressure wasn't on him to perform.

The film was important personally to Francis Ford Coppola, being the tale of a rivalry between two brothers – played by Matt Dillon and Mickey Rourke. Coppola dedicated the back-and-white movie to his brother – and Nicolas's father – August, 'my first and best teacher'. Nic enjoyed being on a Coppola project where the pressure was off. 'It was interesting. Francis asked me to rehearse some actors. So, I wasn't auditioning, I was there reading Matt Dillon and Mickey Rourke.'

What he didn't realise was that Francis was sizing up his acting opposite those auditioning for the film, hoping to offer him a role in the movie to make up for his disappointment over *The Outsiders*. 'The next day I found out I had a job,' said Nic of his unconscious audition for *Rumble Fish*. 'It really blew my mind. That was really high pressure. Here I was, the nephew of the director, without any more under my belt to speak of and that made the other actors nervous. I felt this pressure to pull it off. When I look back, I think it is one of the better things I've done.'

Rumble Fish was a serious 'brat pack' movie, an underrated throw back to the 'rebel' films of James Dean, packed with skilful performances from a series of rising stars, including Rourke, Dillon, Sean Penn's brother Christopher (to feature in *Reservoir Dogs* much later), Diane Lane and Vincent Spano. Rourke played Motorcycle Boy, a legendary gang leader who had left town, and Dillon was his upstart younger brother Rusty James. Dennis Hopper played the brothers' drunken and violent father. Nicolas Cage won the role of Smokey, Rusty James's buddy who succeeds in stealing his girlfriend (Diane Lane) away.

Shot in atmospheric monochrome, the film is loaded with symbolism to reflect the tension and battles between the two brothers, filtered through Coppola's own ambiguous relationship with his brother August. It was an influence that was very clear to Nic, in the most uncomfortable way. 'In my Uncle Francis' imagination my role was very like my father, so he had me sort of looking like him and that was uncomfortable,' he complained shortly afterwards. 'I was terrified, but at that time I didn't know how to say "no". He wouldn't let me create my own thoughts for the character.' Most symbolic are the 'rumble' fish themselves, Siamese fighting fish, dropped into the black and white movie in glorious colour. The fish are unable to co-exist with their siblings, or even with an image of themselves. *Variety* hailed the performances, while feeling the symbolism was heavy and overdone: 'an examination of teenage alienation . . . good performances . . . overwrought and overthought but beautifully photographed'.

Although he was the director's nephew, Nic didn't have an easy ride on *Rumble Fish*, despite what some of the other cast members may have feared. Ever the perfectionist, Coppola had him repeat a simple scene where he glances at his watch over forty times, aiming to get it just right. Nic also experienced some tension with Matt Dillon, who had taken his role in *The Outsiders*, and whom he dubbed 'an airhead'. It was an off-the-cuff comment he was to regret uttering in later years. 'I don't think of Matt Dillon as an airhead,' he later said, making up for his earlier candour. 'He's a darn good actor. The funny thing about growing up in the movies is when you start acting at seventeen you say things sometimes like a seventeen-year-old and those things come back to haunt you when you're older. People have to be allowed to grow.'

After *Rumble Fish* it was time for Nic to stand on his own two feet. The film had been good for him, giving him a solid, visible role, and moving him up from the 21st in the cast list of *Fast Times At Ridgemont High* to 7th. However, it had not been a great economic success, grossing only $2.5 million in the United States. However, for what was effectively a small art film, it was not bad. What Nic needed now was a leading role, an opportunity to strut his stuff away from the guidance of Francis Ford Coppola.

He got his chance with *Valley Girl*, a teen romance movie which owed a lot to *Romeo And Juliet*. The film was directed by Martha Coolidge, who invited Nic to audition knowing he'd had a featured role in *Rumble Fish* but not knowing he was a Coppola. The part was a James Dean-type rebel teen – right up his street – named Randy. Starring opposite him was Deborah Foreman playing Julie, a Valley teen who has split from her high school athlete boyfriend Tommy (Michael Bowen). She meets Randy, and is faced with making a choice between the two. This being a satire, the

A publicity shot of Nic Cage from the teen romance movie Valley Girl. *It was his first leading role.*

less than glamorous Nicolas Cage won out. Nic felt being surrounded by women helped his performance. 'Women see more in me,' he claimed. 'They bring out more, releasing energy stored up. There are things a woman director can see that a male director doesn't, which is new for a male actor. It's fresh and intuitive. Martha really relaxed me . . . This could have been a real take-yourself-seriously teenage role, but she kept encouraging my comic instincts. It's an honest little film.'

Nic's participation in the film wasn't guaranteed after his first reading of the screenplay, though. 'When I first saw that script, the title turned me right off, 'cause if there was one thing in America I really hated it was the "valley girls" in my own high school. Real bimbos, y'know. [Martha] was so determined to show something about teen society. The studio expected a formula exploiter, but because of Martha it came out different.' The difference, according to Cage, was that Coolidge saw some serious social issues under the trappings of the teen movie she'd been handed to make. 'Once I was able to say to a Valley girl "Look, it's not what your friends think, it's not the price tags on your clothes, it's you and me, damn it." It may have been stylised, but at least we did deal with class and social barriers a little.'

Preparing for the role, Nicolas decided he had to get rid of some of the copious amounts of body hair nature had seen fit to lumber him with. 'What happened? Did evolution leave me behind or something? What is going on?' he asked of his hirsute state. Determined to achieve 'that *Superman* look' of a neat V-shape of chest hair he got out the razor and began to shave ruthlessly.

Coolidge didn't care one way or another how he prepared for the role, she was just surprised to find out she'd hired one of the Coppola family, claiming that if she'd known who Nicolas was before casting him it would have 'coloured' her view, just as he'd always suspected. He'd succeed, though, in a leading role and he celebrated by cruising Sunset Boulevard in L.A. in a yellow Triumph Spitfire, blasting out the Beatles' 'Baby, You're A Rich Man'.

As he was taking on a leading role, Nicolas hired a publicity agent to handle his press duties. He wasn't fond of giving interviews, but was smart enough to realise that he had to push both the film and himself, and also that when people realised he was related to Francis Ford Coppola the inevitable questions would have to be answered. He was in no mood to handle them, so hired Ilene Feldman to face the music. 'He didn't want to capitalise on the Coppola name,' noted Feldman. 'He thought it was extremely unfair that people mentioned it. Of course they would – he was a little naive then. But he was young. He signed on with me under the name Nicolas Cage.'

With *Valley Girl* completed, he had his first taste of leading man acclaim, although it was for his unusual features and strange looks that he was singled out, not any particular acting prowess. Reviewers found him difficult to describe, with people coming up with phrases like 'hangdog expression', 'sleepy eyed' and even 'dopey sexuality'. Nic didn't care – he'd played a leading part in a not particularly great film, but it had served his purpose. *Valley Girl* got Nicolas Cage noticed.

'After *Valley Girl* there was a tremendous amount of interest in him,' Ilene Feldman said. 'He seemed to be being bought up for every project that was around. His money went up, but he didn't want to acknowledge his new popularity. He was still insecure.' He didn't fall into the standard brat pack roles, though, which had trapped actors like Rob Lowe and Andrew McCarthy and many of his contemporaries from *Fast Times At Ridgemont High*. 'I never looked young enough to get into teen pix,' he lamented. 'When I met [director] John Hughes he asked me, "How old are you – 35?"'

Although he was new on the professional acting scene, Cage could see around him a group of young actors who he felt were following in the experimental footsteps of his Hollywood idols James Dean and Marlon Brando. 'There was a sort of convergence of young actors from our generation,' he remembered of the early eighties. 'I think we entered an experimental phase of acting, one that may have been made viable through that whole "stylised but streetwise" thing Brando started in the fifties and Robert DeNiro resuscitated. People like Tom Cruise and Sean Penn cared about their work. They were less teen idols, more young fresh talent. My approach was to fuse the darker side with comedy. It's important to go crazy, and never paint with just one brush.' It was to be a philosophy which would fuel his acting approach for several years to come.

With Julie (Deborah Foreman), the eponymous 'valley girl' who dumps her high school athelete boyfriend for Nic's James Dean-type rebel.

Nicolas Cage's worries about attending auditions returned as requests to read for more movies came in to his agent. In a panic, he turned down many of them, finally agreeing to read for a movie called *Racing With The Moon*, and then only because he was likely to co-star in the film with his friend Sean Penn, spreading the risk of failure.

Racing With The Moon was a period piece. Set in 1942, it tells the story of two high school buddies passing the time in the weeks before they join the Marines and go off to take part in the war. Producer Sherry Lansing – who had been the head of film studio 20th Century Fox – had already cast Sean Penn as one half of the duo, and she had definite ideas about who she wanted for the other half. 'I had seen *Valley Girl* and thought Nic had just the right look and feel for Nicky in the Movie. Sean [Penn] is a strong character and we needed someone who wouldn't be overshadowed by him. He had to be a buffer, but also have his own energy. We – and certainly the critics – never complained about the casting.'

Nicolas was Nicky and Penn played Hopper, best friends who've grown up together in the isolated town of Point Muir. The war in Europe has been raging for several years, but it's only now that the pair are old enough to be enlisted to fight. They're leaving behind relationships with friends and loved ones in various states of repair. Hopper comes from a happy family background and he's reluctant to leave his girlfriend (Elizabeth McGovern) behind. Nicky has more reason for wanting to escape to Europe – his mother is dead and he's being abused by his violent father. His girlfriend (Julie Philips) has announced she's pregnant, and the pair want to secure an abortion as they're not ready to be parents. The finished film is a slice-of-life drama, if a bit soap opera-like in places. Directed by actor-turned-journeyman-director Richard Benjamin, *Racing With The Moon* features some neat scenes of action and romance, which pepper the otherwise inconsequential storyline. It also has some notable bit part appearances from actors who would go on to become bigger stars, like *Wayne's World*'s Dana Carvey and *Back To The Future*'s Crispin Glover, whom Nic had gone to school with at Beverly Hills High and who'd also featured in his failed TV pilot *The Best Of Times*.

The elements all seemed right for *Racing With The Moon*, but it was to have a troubled production history. Director Richard Benjamin had been acclaimed the previous year for his Peter O'Toole-starrer *My Favourite Year*, the stars were on the rise and it was to be the first film for the Jaffe-Lansing company, formed by producer Stanley Jaffe (*Kramer Versus Kramer*) and Sherry Lansing. In spite of these attractive elements, the film suffered a series of postponements, sudden hold-ups and last-minute rescues before shooting could finally begin.

Steve Kloves's screenplay had begun life under David Begelman at United Artists, but when he was fired, so too was the script. Submitted to other studios, it was rejected as being too 'soft' and uncommercial, relying more on character and drama than high-concept jeopardy and gadgets, which were just beginning to dominate contemporary cinema thanks to the success of George Lucas and Steven Spielberg. Finally the script reached Sherry Lansing while she was still head of 20th Century Fox. She loved it and purchased it for production. Just one week later she

'The nerd from Fast Times *can actually act,' Sean Penn said to Nic Cage while making* Racing With The Moon.

left Fox after three years to set up as an independent producer, taking the script with her. Fox agreed to still make the film, but at a greatly reduced budget than that originally proposed by Lansing. That upset the other co-producers and the whole project shifted from Fox to Paramount where the Jaffe–Lansing company had a production agreement, just ten days before principal photography was due to begin.

'Paramount gave us an extra week to prepare,' recalled producer Alain Bernheim, a former Parisian literary agent who'd championed the script at all its studio homes over the months. 'They allotted Dick [director Richard Benjamin] four more days to shoot and raised the budget from $6 million to $6.5 million. On a period film, even that little bit extra helps.'

The problems were not over. The producers wanted Sean Penn in the leading role and he wanted to play the part, but he was then starring in the mildly successful Broadway version of *Slab Boys*. With an actors strike also looming, Paramount wanted to start on *Racing With The Moon* right away, with or without Penn. As it happened, Paramount were also financial backers of *Slab Boys*, and in a bizarre bit of business practice, they pulled their funding, causing the play to close, freeing Penn for *Racing With The Moon* and his *Slab Boys* co-star Kevin Bacon to star in their own film, *Footloose*.

Racing With The Moon was ideal casting for both Nic Cage and Sean Penn. They'd already worked together on *Fast Times At Ridgemont High*, and they'd often hang out together in bars in Los Angeles, so their easy rapport as best friends onscreen came naturally. There was an element of competition, too. 'I remember

Nic and Sean Penn became close friends during the shooting of Racing With The Moon. *Cage described Penn as 'an inspirational figure'.*

Sean saying "The nerd from *Fast Times* can actually act!" . . . and we became friends,' remembered Nicolas. 'There's one shot where Sean and I are standing in front of an [oncoming] train and have to jump out of the way at the right time. We got into this stand-off – who was going to jump first? It was good natured but definitely a macho, boys'-day-out attitude between us.'

'I have the utmost respect for Sean,' said Nicolas of the actor whom he regarded as 'an inspirational figure': 'Working with him and watching how he handled his life and career, I think that gave me a handle on how to deal with things, with the pressure.' Just as he was getting cold feet about acting in Hollywood after *Valley Girl*, working with a close friend in reassuring circumstances was just the pick-me-up that Nicolas needed.

Filming began on 2 May 1983, with Cage and Penn based in Northern California for six weeks' location shooting. The coast line of Mendocino was a significant one for Nic – it had been used in his favourite film *East Of Eden* for the opening scenes when James Dean arrives at a coastal town in search of his mother. Being up there got him away from Los Angeles and the pressures of the star system. Although California is the most populated state in America, that area remained fairly isolated. There was no train service, only a daily bus out of Mendocino making the four-hour trip to San Francisco.

The first thing to be done on location was returning the area to the look it had in the early forties. Locals filled the sidewalks as returning servicemen, late-thirties model cars were dotted around, and the Mendocino Bank of America branch was given a false front to stand in as the library from which Hopper (Penn) distributes books to wounded servicemen in the local trauma centre. So convincing was the false frontage that confused locals tried to gain access to the new public amenity they thought had arrived in their midst. The town of Fort Bragg, about seven miles further north of Mendocino, was the location of the malt shop where the high school students would gather after class, as well as of the local movie house featured in the film. The false front on the movie house also impressed the local residents, to such an extent that they kept it after the film-makers had left, using it as the entrance to their recreation centre.

The isolation in Northern California suited Nic down to the ground. The competitive nature of Hollywood sometimes got him down, and reminded him of his not-so-jolly days at school. 'A lot of the problems I have with Hollywood are the same ones I had at high school – it's basically a popularity contest. It's all about who's going out with whom, who's the prettiest, who's the funniest, who's the best.'

When the film was finished and screened to a lukewarm response from critics and the public, Nic had a ready explanation for its poor $5.4 million gross takings. 'I didn't think it was that good,' he claimed, laying the blame at the door of the inexperienced director. 'Richard Benjamin, who is really an actor, was too new at his craft. The film looked great because he spent time on the technical aspects of it, rather than on the actors. Consequently, my character was terribly incomplete.'

He also felt the film was too wishy-washy in its approach to the subject matter to capture much attention. 'I felt it was something of a Hallmark Card – sweet and sentimental without any depth or danger . . . The danger I tried to bring to it seemed to come from nowhere, since Richard Benjamin failed to point up the emotional background which led my character to behave like that about getting the girl pregnant. I came off looking like a jerk; he let me down.' Nic's frank criticisms of the film, made shortly after its release, showed he was to be more than just an actor-for-hire. Instead, he had a deep emotional involvement in his films and wished to make them the best he possibly could. It was an approach that would lead to constant improvisation, self-direction and an interest in what was happening behind the camera as well as an involvement in what was going on in front of the lens.

'I had this dream of six years of studying before I started working,' claimed Cage of his burst of career development at the time of *Racing With The Moon*. 'Instead, I've done three films in a year. It's scary, but exciting.'

3. Acting Up

WITH FOUR FILMS UNDER HIS belt and a new identity, Nicolas Cage was nonetheless still finding it difficult to win acting roles. Neither *Valley Girl* nor *Racing With The Moon* had made a huge impact, although they'd done enough to get him established. His best work to date had been *Rumble Fish,* and that had been courtesy of his Uncle Francis.

With that in mind, when he was offered another role by Francis in *The Cotton Club,* Nicolas overcame his worries about nepotism and jumped at the chance, despite being warned off by his publicity manager. Ilene Feldman told the actor that working with his uncle again so soon would provoke accusations once again that he only won the role through his family connections. Nic overcame this reservation by approaching his acting roles in a more relaxed manner than he had started out with. 'Although *Rumble Fish* was my first taste of feature films, it wasn't a good experience for me,' he admitted. 'It filled me with far more tension than I think I needed on my first outing, and it wasn't until *Valley Girl* that I really understood that you could relax and take it easy. After *Valley Girl* came out, Francis became very excited and wanted to work with me again, on *The Cotton Club*, but I wasn't so sure.'

The producer and author of *The Godfather,* Robert Evans and Mario Puzo, had reunited for this tale of gangsters and jazz set in and around a twenties Harlem club. Evans was a high-profile notorious Hollywood figure, who had risen from being a matinee idol actor to become a successful producer and reputed womaniser in the seventies through to running Paramount Studios and saving it from bankruptcy.

Setting out with the best of intentions for the film, Coppola and Evans would eventually produce a costly flop which turned out to be a dangerous film to have been involved with. Stories surrounding the film involved real-life gangsters, allegations that drug money was funding it, and even a murder mystery. Robert Evans was ostracised by the Hollywood film-making community when the press implicated him in what became known as '*The Cotton Club* murder'.

The troubles lay in the financing of the film. Evans had optioned the rights in 1980 for a mere $350,000, intending to produce and direct himself. In later years he raised a further $8 million on the basis of a poster and a tagline ('*The Godfather* with music!') promoting the as yet unmade film. All he needed was a further $12 million and he could make the film without studio involvement. That's when things began to go seriously wrong for him.

His first financial partners on the project were the Khashoggi Brothers, well-known Arab investors, who put up $1 million for Mario Puzo to write the screenplay, and offered a further $12 million on the basis that Evans would mortgage his Hollywood Hills home as security. Evans refused and the deal fell apart. It looked like *The Cotton Club* was history, until another pair of brothers – Ed and Fred Doumanu, casino owners from Las Vegas – in association with Victor Sayyah, an investor from Denver, financed Puzo's script and put up the money for the film.

At the same time, Evans embarked on an ambitious project to raise funding for his own film-making company. He fell into bad company, making a deal with drug-trafficking couple Roy Radin and Laney Jacobs Greenberger for $50 million. Before the details of the deal were fully worked out, Radin had been murdered, his body turning up in a quarry. While the police investigated, *The Cotton Club* had suddenly caught on in Hollywood in a big way, becoming something of a hot property. Paramount offered Richard Gere as one of the stars, while Orion offered to fund the production, but gave Evans full artistic control. The only problem was Puzo's script – Orion didn't like it.

While considering Richard Gere for the lead, Evans believed in 1982 he had Sylvester Stallone lined up for a role. 'Stallone wanted desperately to do the film,' Evans told *MovieLine* magazine. 'During that period he was making *Rocky 3*. He used to come over and try on hats to see how he'd look in the picture. Later I'm in Cannes with 300 distributors to sell *The Cotton Club* and I get a call from Sly at 2 a.m.' Stallone told Evans he didn't like the script and wanted out of the film. Evans was furious as that coming morning he was pitching the movie at Cannes with Stallone attached as the star. But despite having no screenplay and no leading actor, Evans pitched the movie to distributors anyway and sold rights worth $8 million in 45 minutes, based on the poster alone. Evans and Stallone never reconciled after the casting incident.

With the police still looking into the mysterious death of Roy Radin, Evans hired Coppola for $2.5 million to direct and rewrite Puzo's screenplay. The Doumani brothers pulled out of the film when it became clear that Puzo's work was to be dumped. With money running out and the New York studio space which had been booked costing him $140,000 each week, Evans allegedly used money from his putative film company deal with Laney Jacobs Greenberger and the late Roy Radin to plug the cash flow gap. Evans denied drawing on the drug money for the film. 'I didn't need the money,' he claimed. 'I already had the money. I had to get $2 million to pay the weekly payroll. Money was due to me from Orion the following Thursday, but money had to be paid that Friday. I went to four men to ask them for the loan, guaranteed by Orion the following Thursday, and all four – for each of whom I had made $100 million or more – gave me excuses why they couldn't give it to me. The first two women I went to gave it to me before I'd finished the

The Godfather *with music' was how producer Robert Evans sold* The Cotton Club, *Nicolas Cage's second film with his uncle Francis Ford Coppola.*

sentence, and asked me if I wanted more – Liv Ullman and Cheryl Tiegs.'

The funding crisis and alleged involvement of drug dealers resulted in the arrival of one Joey Cusomano, replacing Evans as producer of the film. Rumours flew that Cusomano was 'connected', a Mafia kingpin, using the production to launder 'dirty' money. Evans' financier Laney Jacobs Greenberger was then arrested for arranging the murder of her partner Roy Radin, and as a financial partner of both, Evans became the centre of media attention. The press covered the case in sensational terms, although it wasn't until 1989 that it came to trial and Evans took the Fifth Amendment to avoid having to testify. It was alleged that although Evans himself had not been directly involved in the murder, Laney Jacobs Greenberg was said to have confessed to the producer that she had arranged for the 'hit' as part of a dispute over drug money. Evans's name was mud in Hollywood as a result.

In the middle of all this chaos it was all but impossible for Coppola to keep control of his set. Evans had hoped to recreate *The Godfather* success by hiring the same director, and Coppola quickly set about redrafting the script to reflect his concerns, echoing the emphasis on sibling relationships that were at the centre of *Rumble Fish*.

The film became something of a Coppola clan outing, with Francis directing, Nicolas Cage taking one of the four central roles, and Coppola's sons Gian-Carlo

'By the time I was on film, I truly believed I was a psychotic whack job gangster thug.'

and Roman working as production assistants (as they had been on their father's *Rumble Fish*). None of them – despite their experience – were prepared for the troubled production process they found themselves involved in.

Robert Evans was clear on what he wanted the movie to be: '*The Godfather* with music – music, sex and gangsters.' For Coppola, though, things were more complicated. He'd already made a musical with *Finian's Rainbow*, and here was a chance to combine that with a classy throwback to the Warner Brothers gangster pictures of the thirties and forties that featured James Cagney and Edward G. Robinson. 'It has music and it has theatre, great theatre, and beautiful dancers. I made it clear that if I had control there was no reason why I couldn't make a beautiful film out of it,' said Coppola.

Family was at the centre of the film as Coppola envisaged it. Richard Gere played Dixie Dwyer, a cornet player who lands on his feet when he saves the life of Mob boss Dutch Schultz, only to fall for Schultz's girlfriend Vera Cicero (Coppola regular Diane Lane). Nicolas Cage was Gere's would-be gangster brother. Gregory Hines struggled with the role of dancer Sandman William, who's working for the Mob while hoping to become a star.

Filming had begun without a final script – there were to be 39 versions, all on different coloured paper, giving it the nickname 'the rainbow script'. Gere was the most expensive member of the cast, costing Evans and Coppola $3 million, with a further $125,000 each week he remained on set beyond the original wrap date of 30 October 1983. While the financial arrangement made it possible for Gere to control his frustrations, the same could not be said of Nicolas Cage.

Having agreed to the role hoping to advance his career, Nic found himself hanging around waiting for something to happen. His anger increased as the weeks passed and he watched the film fall apart around him in a sea of Mob money and cocaine. Fulfilling his James Dean complex, he fell into the part of the bad-boy film star and trashed his trailer, taking out his anger on the furniture and contents. 'I was very frustrated on *The Cotton Club*. I was slated for three weeks' work. I was there for six months, in costume, in make-up, on the set in case Francis got an idea that would involve my character. Meanwhile, I'm getting offers of starring roles in other movies and I can't do them. So my behaviour – all the acting out – came from frustration. I was young and behaving like a guy who listened to early Who music and wanted to be a rebel, a punk rocker. I didn't really know how to act, so I took a "method" approach. I was trying to be like my heroes, like Robert DeNiro.'

Richard Gere was more experienced in the ways of Hollywood, and saw the delays and frustration as part of the movie-making process. He gave Nic some advice after his trailer-trashing antics. 'You keep going like this and you're only going to have five more movies in you,' he warned the rising star.

Furniture was not the only thing Nic smashed when playing out his frustrations during the making of *The Cotton Club*. An innocent street vendor of remote-control cars found himself the target of his wrath as the angry actor jumped on his wares. 'I wasn't having fun in those days,' claimed Cage, looking back to his early method antics. 'I look back and see that my whole acting process was coming from pain, right up until *Peggy Sue Got Married*. In *Birdy*, I was in pain. On *The Cotton Club* I was inflicting pain. I would walk down Christopher Street and say, "How much for that remote-control car?", then I'd lift it up, throw it on the pavement and smash it. Everybody would scatter and think I was crazy. Then I went back to my trailer and ripped it up, threw the mattress out the window, threw the lamp out the window. Man, people thought I had lost my mind. The character was racist, so I'd stalk around calling everybody "nigger". By the time I was on film, I truly believed I was a psychotic whack job gangster thug. Needless to say, I was rather disliked.'

Cage was out of his element on *The Cotton Club*, despite – or perhaps because of – the fact that he was working with his uncle. 'I felt like a fish out of water,' he recalled. 'I was really lost. I didn't know the city, I didn't have a script, and I didn't know what work I was going to be doing on what day. I was in a constant state of confusion and I worried a lot because of that. I think Francis made a good film, but I would never have thought that would be the end result because of the lack of team-work and unity on the picture. None of the other actors were having a good time either. Spontaneity may have been his aim and probably it worked, but having everyone present on the set in case he had an idea didn't please many people.'

Robert Evans has now put the experience of *The Cotton Club*, his conviction for cocaine use and his gangster involvement behind him. 'Everything about *The Cotton Club* went wrong. Al Pacino had turned down the lead. Sylvester Stallone took it and then dropped out and it was eventually a critical and commercial belly flop. It was one of those projects where nothing would go right. It was an evil and difficult time for me. Hollywood is full of stories about movies like *The Cotton Club*. No one said making movies was easy.'

The film failed at the box office, taking slightly over $26 million in the United States, resulting in a loss of about $38 million against the production costs. *Box Office* magazine noted its problems: 'It's a lavish entertainment, but it's also a movie without a centre. It has some wonderfully funny moments and a whole gallery of great supporting characters,' wrote Jimmy Summers. 'Much has been written about producer Robert Evans' trials in getting *The Cotton Club* to the screen and the manner in which Coppola created the script as he went along. Sad to say, all of that shows up in the improvised feeling and inconsistencies of the finished product.' Despite the commercial failure of the film, there was some serious critical acclaim. *The Cotton Club* was nominated for Golden Globes for Best Picture and Best Director. That was followed by two Oscar nominations – one for editing, one for art direction and set decoration. Unfortunately actress Diane Lane was also singled out, this time for a Razzie Award as the Worst Supporting Actress of the year.

Despite his age and his appearance in the teen movie *Fast Times At Ridgemont High*, Nicolas Cage was never a fully fledged member of the 'brat pack', that loose grouping of pretty young Hollywood types who emerged in the early to mid-eighties. 'It's not that I consciously avoided it,' he claimed, 'it's more that I wasn't invited into it. I wasn't allowed to be a member. I tried to get into some of those movies, but . . .' Among their number were Demi Moore (the only one to go on to superstar status), Charlie Sheen, his brother Emilio Estevez, Andrew McCarthy, Rob Lowe, Molly Ringwald, Ally Sheedy and Matthew Broderick. Nic knew them all, and occasionally hung out with them, when he wasn't on a drinking session with Sean Penn, but he didn't think of himself as 'one of them'. He thought of himself as being much more in line with classic movie rebels Marlon Brando and James Dean. So fixated on these screen icons was he that he had begun acting like them off screen in real life, as his trailer-trashing outburst during the making of *The Cotton Club* showed.

'I was trying to create a mythology around myself,' he recalls now. 'All my heroes had stories about them, whether they were true or false. I learned that you can't have a life if you lived the part – but then I wanted to generate stories about myself. I had an adolescent energy that was geared towards punk rock or that rebellious rock 'n' roll image. I had heard tall tales about idols and icons I admired and I bought into the lore.'

His friend Jim Carrey – later to win fame as the star of *The Mask*, *Ace Ventura* and as the Riddler in *Batman Forever* – recalled life around Cage when he was

Alan Parker directs Nic Cage and Matthew Modine in Birdy, *his anti-realist movie about the Vietnam war.*

aspiring to be a Hollywood wild man. 'When we first hung out, he was a little crazy, a little frivolous – raw emotion coming out everywhere, with a lot of anger. He was occasionally embarrassing to be around.'

Motorcycles became a passion of this would-be Wild One, but while he did speed around town on the back of a bike, it was more of an image thing than a real passion. 'The motorcycle thing got out of hand,' Nicolas has admitted. 'I was feeling restless, and I happened to see *Easy Rider* and thought: "Yeah, I have to go get a motorcycle." I like Mickey Rourke [his *Rumble Fish* co-star], but I never once rode motorcycles with him.' Rather than doing the biker act at after-hours clubs, Nic was more likely to be caught in class at UCLA during this period studying wine, an interest he'd picked up when staying at the Napa winery with his uncle.

Getting a tattoo was also part of Nic's Hollywood rebellion phase. He acquired an eight-inch one of a lizard on his shoulder, but in his typically offbeat and humorous style the lizard is wearing a top hat. 'I had a stupid rationalisation – I would never have to take my shirt off in a movie again – at a time when I felt I could have fallen into the trap of being the "beefcake hunk". More important, I was claiming my own body and my own right as a man over myself in circumstances where my father would see it. When he did, he went "Oh my God" and his face turned white. It was a good moment – like a metamorphosis.' Of all his roles, his tattoo was most visible in *Moonstruck*. Along with changing his name, Nicolas had set out to change his body, too. Later, he'd buy a real lizard as a pet, and he named it Smokey after his character in *Rumble Fish*.

British film director Alan Parker had never been afraid of controversy. He had come to film-making through advertising, one of a group of British directors who found success in Hollywood in the mid-eighties, including brothers Ridley and Tony Scott, Hugh Hudson and Adrian Lynne. Parker had given Jodie Foster an early role as a gangster's moll in his film *Bugsy Malone*, which featured children in all the roles. Genre-hopping became his trademark, from the drama and controversy of *Midnight Express* to the musical *Fame*, from Faustian horror in *Angel Heart* to race-relations in *Mississippi Burning*. It seemed inevitable that he'd make a Vietnam movie at some point, but with *Birdy* he would take a distinctively unique approach.

Based on William Wharton's allegorical novel, *Birdy* featured Nicolas Cage as a Vietnam veteran who strives to help a childhood friend (Matthew Modine) who has been driven insane by his experiences in the war and mutely believes himself to be a bird. Glossy and packed with striking images, Parker's anti-realist Vietnam movie was saved from arty irrelevance by the strengths of the two central performances. One of these gave Nic his first real chance to stand on his own in an important movie that didn't see him propped up by his uncle.

Birdy *was packed with striking images.*

For his role in *Birdy*, Nic dived with a vengeance into the world of method acting, determined to force himself to experience something he could use to portray a facially scarred Vietnam veteran, a character he had no personal experience of. Discovering he required some dental work to remove two prominent baby teeth which had not come out naturally, Nic arranged for the surgery to coincide with his starting work on the film. 'You know, pulling your teeth out is not living the part of a Vietnam veteran,' he admitted, 'but in my nineteen-year-old brain I was trying to do whatever I could. I remember I dismantled the script and put all the monologues on my hotel room wall. I'd get out of bed in the morning with bandages still on my face because I never took them off. I was trying to lose all this weight. I really beat myself up for that part. And when I saw the movie, I thought, "Well, gosh, I didn't give it enough thought or shadings". I referred to it as emotional vomit. But I look at it now and I feel better about it.'

Nicolas didn't study acting and he certainly didn't have an acting guru or tutor to push him in the direction of the method approach. It was something he developed for himself, a seemingly natural approach for him to understand and get under the skin of the characters he was to play. 'It was my idea to have the teeth pulled and to wear the bandages,' he confirmed. 'It gave me the right "feel". If you work honestly in one direction, you'll find that other directions are taken care of on their own. Because of the bandages my jaw always hurt, which in turn made it difficult for me to eat, so I lost 15 pounds. My mental attitude to the part had helped me to alter physically.'

It was a serious approach to a serious role, even if the press were later to present Nicolas's actions as if they were some form of temporary madness, as though he were suffering from some variation on the mental afflictions that had affected his mother. It was more important to Nic, though, to get a firm grip on the reality of his character. 'The teeth thing was going a little far,' he later admitted. 'The bandages were valuable to me. I would see people's reactions and understand what it must be like for someone in that situation.'

Nicolas struck up a lasting friendship with his *Birdy* co-star Matthew Modine. The pair got together before shooting for a 'get-to-know-you' burger and fries. It was just as well they got on as, according to Nic, director Alan Parker left them very much to their own devices when it came to building their characters for the film. 'He was very set on the script and he didn't like to discuss the characters very much,' recalled Nic of making *Birdy*. 'He made it clear that it was up to the two of us to deliver, to come up with the ideas and the motives for the characters, but that in the end it was him who decided yes or no.'

Looking back on the film Nic later felt he'd gone too far in his method madness. 'It's hard for me to watch it,' he admits of his ground breaking performance. 'I feel like I'm giving too much away, there's no mystery there. Basically, I was still inexperienced and that was a very complex and dramatic role. I went gung-ho for it without putting too much thought behind it. I'd call it jacking off, I guess.'

However, his method approach paid off handsomely. Showing at the Cannes

Film Festival, Parker's affecting film won a twelve-minute standing ovation and scooped the sought-after Grand Jury Prize. It was the first award for a film featuring Nicolas Cage.

With *Birdy*, Nic had finally fulfilled some of the serious promise he had shown in *Rumble Fish*, but offscreen he was still determined to play hard. One of his off-screen pals was a young would-be rock star called Johnny Depp. Depp had been married to guitarist Lori Ann Alison, but they were divorced after just over a year together. Alison had then begun going out with an up-and-coming actor: twenty-year-old Nicolas Cage. Surprisingly, Cage and Depp became friends, and the pair would spend many evenings together in the drinking dens of Sunset Strip. 'It was difficult for me to make friends,' Nic admitted of his early years as a working actor. 'I met Johnny Depp playing Monopoly in a club. I'd been seeing his ex-girlfriend. At first we didn't like each other, but then we did and I told him he should be an actor.'

Depp had come to Los Angeles with his band the Kids, hoping to make it big in the music world, but he was going nowhere fast. Hanging out with Nic, a change of direction was proposed. 'I always thought it would be cool to act,' claimed Depp, 'but it was my friend Nicolas Cage who tried to talk me into giving it a go. I was walking down Melrose Avenue looking for a job, when I bumped into Nic and his agent. Three days later I met Wes Craven.' As a result of Nic's encouragement, Depp went up for an audition for one of the leading teen roles in a proposed stalk 'n' slash chiller named *A Nightmare On Elm Street*. He won the part and made such an impact that he went on to build a successful career as a distinctive and individualistic actor.

The relationship between Lori Ann Alison and Nicolas Cage didn't even last as long as her year with Depp. Nic was young and enjoying the first fruits of success in the movies, and he found it easy to strike up relationships of varying lengths with a variety of women. Among them were Ami Dolenz, daughter of sixties pop star Mickey Dolenz of the Monkees and one-time TV presenter Samantha Just. However, it was a young actress named Jenny Wright who tamed his developing wild side, at least for a while. She had featured on the daytime soap opera *General Hospital*, and later won parts in *Young Guns 2* and cyberthriller *The Lawnmower Man*.

'I find women utterly mysterious,' Nicolas admitted. 'Things happen between a man and a woman that are mysterious. I don't really understand why I am attracted to a woman. Love can do more damage than anger if it goes wrong. Anger passes quickly, but love, when unrequited or ignored, is devastating. However, if it is received and returned it is a magnifying glass to everything that is beautiful in the world.'

Nic relied heavily on method acting for
his role as a facially scarred war veteran in Birdy.

Nic and Jenny Wright shared a flat in Hollywood, staying together for almost three years. Nic furnished the apartment like scenes in his beloved *Batman* comic-books. 'If you were to open up a thirties *Batman* comic-book, you'd see the furniture Bruce Wayne was sitting in. I tried to copy that drawing,' he said. It was an odd relationship, with Wright living constantly with her fears that Nic would take up the opportunity of relationships with his female co-stars. 'My relationships have been tumultuous,' admitted Nicolas of his love life. 'It's all the trials and tribulations that get me wanting to do something – in fact, it's love that inspires me.' The Wright–Cage relationship was a stormy one, as is so often the case with Hollywood couples. As well as the normal relationship troubles which everyone suffers, the pair were involved in a competitive industry, and Nic's career seemed to be progressing at a pace well ahead of Wright's. It was a constant source of friction, but the pair managed to tough it out, for a while at least.

Although it was not released in Canada and the United States until January 1986, *The Boy In Blue* was made between August and October 1984. Nic went straight from playing an emotional and physical cripple for Alan Parker to personifying a real-life, upright Canadian hero for director Charles Jarrott. He'd had only one day off before arriving in Montreal to begin shooting his new film. 'One of the reasons that I wanted to do it was because I needed a crash course to get me out of that guy in *Birdy.*'

The film was seen, somewhat hopefully, as a Canadian version of *Rocky*, but with a boisterous comic edge. Nicolas, in fake tan and real muscles which he worked on during the making of *Birdy*, played Ned Hanlan, a nineteenth-century adventurer and sailor who became famous as a champion oarsman. 'I was a skinny bag of bones when I started this film,' he said. Arduous training sessions with Olympic sculling champion Atelido Magione soon sorted that out. 'For the first three days I couldn't stand up.' At the end of ten days, Nic had regained the weight he'd lost for *Birdy* and mastered the tricky business of propelling a shallow-bottomed racing shell without tipping over in the water, enabling him to row in all the races in the film.

Although he worked hard on developing his physique for the role, Nic wasn't pleased with the outcome. 'I couldn't begin to explain how painful it was. When I saw that, I thought, "Well, I'm never going to take my shirt off again," or at least, not like that. I wanted to go as far away from the beefcake image as possible. The movies that I made that were mistakes, I always learned something from.'

Although far from faultless, *The Boy In Blue* is an enjoyable little film, a kind of superior TV movie-of-the-week. Nic is charming as the romantic rogue at the centre of a rowing-and-betting scandal, and plays well against his more experienced co-stars, Christopher Plummer and David Naughton. From running a moonshine delivery business, to romancing the ladies and out-rowing his rivals, Nic plays Hanlan as a contemporary figure dropped into a period piece. It's an interesting choice and his good-natured exuberance suits this fine and funny comedy film to a tee.

Despite Nicolas's lack of enthusiasm for the movie, *The Boy In Blue* was something of a hit in Canada, where it took $7.8 million, while only grossing around $250,000 in the US. Unsure of what to do with their odd little movie, the distributors had left it on the shelf for over a year, only releasing the film when *Peggy Sue Got Married* was raising Nicolas's profile significantly. It was reviewed – not altogether favourably – in the *New York Times* by Nina Darnton. She felt 'Cage plays a quality rather than a character – an untutored, boorish sort of lout with a good heart. He doesn't infuse the role with the kind of personal depth or individual detail that would make the character come alive. We are left with an outer shell that seems phoney.'

Most successful Hollywood actors play the same type of part repeatedly. Arnold Schwarzenegger and Sylvester Stallone are muscle-bound action heroes, and it can be difficult for audiences to accept them in comedies – although Arnold has enjoyed more success than Sly. Harrison Ford and Tom Cruise are always going to play good guys who win through in the end, and cinemagoers can be reassured that their performance in their newest film will, by and large, be much the same as the last one. As in so many other aspects of his approach to life, Nicolas Cage was determined to be different on this front, too.

As an new actor learning his craft and feeling his way through the industry, Nic was reluctant to find a niche, a 'type' which he could play and build a career on. He was more interested in experimenting, in the process of acting itself, in creating new, very different characters. After all, he'd invented himself as 'Nicolas Cage' and didn't want to stop trying out new identities yet. 'I tried to change my look, walk and my voice – my voice mainly through low self-esteem,' he said of his early experimentation. 'When you start at an early age you don't have a lot of experience to draw on, you're sort of put in a position where you have to try everything – it's part of the experimenting and the growing.'

However, this approach to the craft of acting didn't do Nicolas any favours with the Hollywood establishment. 'At one time Nic was just a little bit dangerous to be around,' recalled his friend Jim Carrey, who was to work with him on *Peggy Sue Got Married*. 'He was just expressing himself. He'd stare at someone in a really weird way just to see what the reaction was. I'd say, "Well, what are you being psycho for?" He's matured – he's gotten sophisticated about it now.' Nic's choice of roles was also baffling to his advisers and to Hollywood pundits. He was turning down potentially lucrative 'hunk' roles to avoid typecasting and seemed to be indulging in a love-hate relationship with Francis Ford Coppola. Every second movie, he'd return to the Coppola fold for a confidence boost. His acting successes had been with less-than-mainstream material: *Rumble Fish* and *Birdy*. Jim Carrey remembers: 'Everybody I know had whispered in my ear at one point: "He has a lot of talent, but what the fuck is he doing?"'

In 1985 Nicolas was due to take a leading part in a nuclear thriller called *Miracle Mile*, but production problems delayed the film and Nic found himself with a hole in his schedule. He'd also started to dabble in scriptwriting and worked on a comedy screenplay which he hoped he could star in some day. As had happened before, a chance to work again with his Uncle Francis proved too attractive to resist, despite bad memories of his adventures on *The Cotton Club*. 'When I first read *Peggy Sue* I wasn't interested. I turned it down four times,' he said of the co-starring role opposite Kathleen Turner in the time-travel romance. 'Francis kept at me to do the picture and convinced me to take it. He said it would be like *Our Town* [a sprawling human drama about family conflict in a small town from 1940]. He said he really wanted me to be in it.'

The film had been through several hands – like *The Cotton Club* before it – when Coppola got involved. It was his kind of movie, if lighter than some of his other work. 'I think those kind of notions for a film – like a woman who goes back in time – those are the type of fantasies that if they are done with a lot of heart and a little bit of eccentricity so they aren't just the same as every other movie, then there's a place for them,' he said. He replaced Penny Marshall as director, and actress Debra Winger who'd been signed up for the leading role promptly pulled out. Coppola quickly persuaded Kathleen Turner – star of *Body Heat, Romancing The Stone* and *Prizzi's Honor* – to take the lead role of a middle-aged woman whose marriage is on the rocks. She attends her high school reunion, only to find herself magically whisked back in time to the early sixties when she was Queen of the high school prom. Getting the chance to relive her life, can she do it any differently this time around? 'Peggy Sue gets to play with her fate,' said Turner. 'I decided I wanted to do it the minute Francis and I started to sing songs from the era – we had a lot of fun.'

Nic finally agreed to take the role of Charlie Bodel, Turner's appliance-salesman husband. The majority of the role, though, was playing the teenage version of the character, out to sweet-talk his future wife, while she knows the eventual failed outcome of their liaison. 'I saw something there in the hopelessness of the situation,' said Nic of the factor that finally reeled him in to do the movie. 'I like the idea of someone trying to maintain their dignity with the odds totally against them. Imagine dating someone who knows that you will be divorced twenty years later on? Now, that's really a no-win situation.'

Nic was determined – come what may – to play the role his way. 'My character was an adult who goes back to high school, to a time in his life when a guy's voice hasn't necessarily changed yet.' The voice became the key to the character for Nic – and a source of disturbance for everyone else on the film. 'I started doing this way out voice, and people were rolling their eyes and saying "What the hell is going on?" Kathleen Turner was frustrated with me. Here she is in this great star vehicle, directed by a great director and her leading man comes along with buck teeth and ultra-blond hair, talking like Pokey [a clay horse] from *The Gumby Show*. I can understand why she was pissed off. Can you blame her? I was basically working without regard for anyone on the movie, just doing whatever I wanted and hijacking the movie, for better or worse.'

It seemed as if Nic had gone off to star in a different movie from everyone else, abandoning his co-stars to struggle through the original film. The result was strong pressure on Coppola, especially from Turner, to have him fired from the movie. Jim Carrey had a bit part in the film alongside his friend. He saw the pressure for Nic's removal mounting as the days went by and his performance got ever more over-the-top: 'Everybody wanted him fired. Kathleen Turner was not crazy about him. Francis had the producers up to his house for spaghetti, to calm them down. He said to me: "The same thing happened on *The Godfather*. Everybody wanted Brando out of there. He showed up with cotton in his cheeks, and they thought he was making a mockery out of the movie."'

Nic himself has admitted: 'If (Coppola) had not been directing, I would have been fired. It was a weird world. I was very young when I shot *Peggy Sue*. I will stand by that character, but I can see why my playing it that way was frustrating for Kathleen Turner. She had her own vision of what the character was like, and her vision was much more in keeping with everyone else's, and there I was on the set saying: "This guy should be a goofball, he's going to be a nerd." But that was the deal I had with Francis. He said: "I'll let you do it the way you want," so I did.'

Nic claimed to have taken part of the inspiration for his wild, brave and foolhardy performance from the direction that Coppola was pushing the film in anyway. After all, *Peggy Sue Got Married* was a fantasy. 'I saw Francis being very adventuresome, painting the sidewalks pink and the trees yellow and getting surreal. I thought: "Why can't the actors do that?" I had license to do whatever I want, because in dreams you can get as abstract as you want.'

While he was having a blast with his out-there playing, Nicolas didn't realise that Coppola was struggling to keep the film together, especially when it came to placating Turner. After the *Cotton Club* debacle, this was all Coppola needed. 'I don't think she blamed me after she saw the movie,' Nic later recalled of his put-out co-star. 'But while we were making it she was like: "What are you doing? You're ruining the movie!" She was dealing with, what? Jerry Lewis on acid? She said to me: "You know, a film is a permanent record. Be careful what you do!"'

Coppola began production, as he often did, with an extended rehearsal period for his cast – unusual in modern Hollywood. Despite initially feeling it was a waste of time, Kathleen Turner came to welcome the preparation period. 'It was strange at first. It was like acting school with all the improvisation and trust exercises. I was rather impatient, but after a couple of days I realised that people were really getting involved in the process and it was working.'

Shot entirely on location in Sonoma County, just next to Coppola's beloved Napa Valley, filming on *Peggy Sue Got Married* began on 19 August 1985 and wrapped on schedule and to budget in the third week of October. A big challenge for Coppola and his team had been finding locations which were suitable to the period featured in the movie. Petaluma offered almost all of the twenty or so locations all within easy distance of each other, including Peggy Sue's family home and the Bodell appliance shop, which was packed with vintage gadgets. Santa Rosa High School stood in as the location of many of the school scenes.

Despite her fears about Cage's performance, the end result didn't do Kathleen

Turner any harm, however. The film was generally welcomed by critics and she was nominated for an Academy Award. For Nic, the reception was somewhat different. '"A wart on an otherwise beautiful movie!" Most people didn't like me in *Peggy Sue*,' he admitted. 'I thought unless I garnered bad reviews, I wasn't doing my job. I was an arrogant young man who knew that all great artists were always put down for taking chances, so I thought, I have to do something where they put me down, or I'm not doing anything of quality. I'm sure I'm gonna make movies that will piss people off. I read my bad reviews – they're more colourful than the good ones. I used to cut them out and keep them.'

He got plenty of cuttings for the scrap book. The *New Yorker* claimed Nic was simply 'miscast', while *Cosmopolitan* pegged him as being a 'romantic goofball'. He was sanguine at these bad notices. 'Another said I was "A poorly wired robot". I didn't care. I was happy with the result of the movie. A lot of my friends who didn't like it at first now like it. It did well – Kathleen Turner got an Academy Award nomination and it made a lot of money. I got lambasted by the critics.'

The film was re-evaluated in later years and critics came to see Nicolas's eccentric turn as part of a larger project that only became visible in retrospect after he'd made several more movies. However, some contemporary critics were supportive of his maverick turn. The *Chicago Sun-Times*' Roger Ebert was taken by the unorthodox performance, in what he rated as one of the films of the year for 1986. 'We meet him first as a local businessman in his early '40s, and from the way he walks into a room you can tell he's the kind of man who inspires a lot of local gossip. He and his wife are separated and planning to divorce. When we see him again, he's the teenage guy she's dating. There are two delicate, wonderful scenes where she walks a tightrope, trying to relate to him as if she were a teenager, and as if she hadn't already shared his whole future. [One] scene in the front seat of the car is a masterpiece of cross purposes: She actually wants to go all the way, and he's shocked – shocked not so much by her desire, as by a girl having the temerity to talk and act that way in 1960. "Jeez," he says, after she makes her move. "That's a guy's line."'

Washington Post critic Paul Attanasio was another supporter of Nic's gambit: 'Playing opposite Turner, Cage finds his own ingenious solution to the problem of making time travel seem real – he plays Charlie as a stylised version of an early '60s teenager. He affects a Fabian pompadour and a dental insert that makes him look goofy, but the cartoon goes further as Cage twists his voice with a twangy nasality and builds the insecurities of adolescence into the stuttering of Charlie's guffaw. With remarkable detail, Cage locates what's vain and superficial about Charlie (he's the kind of kid who can focus obsessively on a Rice Krispies square), but he also finds what's touching – his confusion, and his dreams about the future. He makes you feel that Charlie's not all that different from Peggy Sue – he's searching for what's important in life, too, but without the benefit of hindsight.'

These good reviews didn't help the overall perception, though. Nicolas Cage was now seen as a goofball of an actor who'd thrown away a chance to make a big impression in a mainstream, successful movie. Instead, he was thought of as a laughing stock. The film was the last one Nic was to make with his Uncle Francis. Although Coppola had given Nic a free hand, he regretted it when the film opened and he saw how Nic's performance was received. 'Francis did blame me,' Nic admitted. 'He hasn't changed his mind about me. I wanted to be in *The Godfather Part 3*. I thought I would have been a more logical choice as Jimmy Caan's son than Andy Garcia. I would have loved to have been in Francis's *Dracula*. Dracula is one of my favourite characters and much of my life is modelled after him. To me Dracula is love in exile – I'm very inspired by that idea.'

Despite Coppola's anger, out there on the fringes of Hollywood there were directors and A-list actresses who were keen to work with this bizarre talent that had appeared in their midst. His approach to acting seemed new and unique and there were people who appreciated what he was trying to do. 'I don't really like to limit myself to reality,' he explained. 'I have more fun. The state of acting around the world is naturalism, but I enjoy other performances, like Dennis Hopper in *Blue Velvet*. To me, that's brave and reminiscent of actors like James Cagney who were large and dynamic. I think that some of that dynamic acting has been lost on account of going for reality. The main thing with me is, I just want to keep trying new things.' His real career was just about to begin.

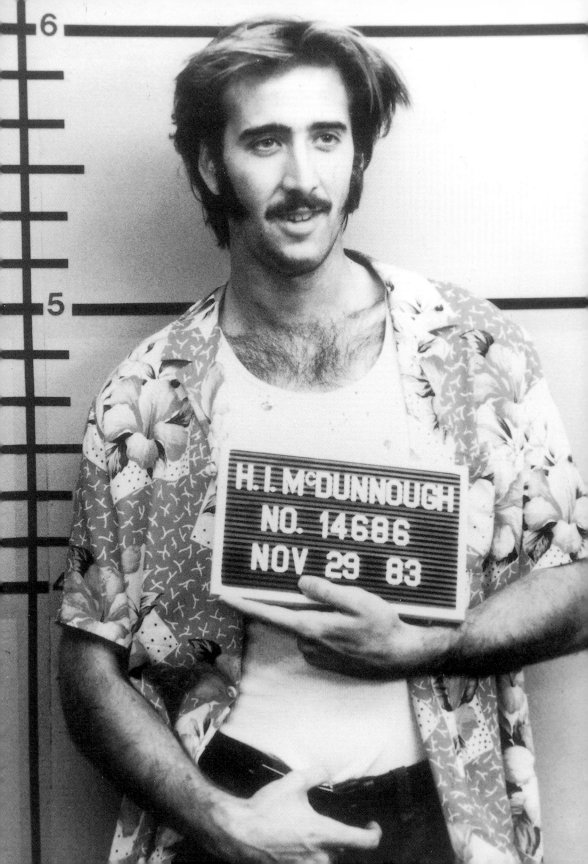

4. Romantic Gestures

B Y 1987, WHEN HE WAS 23 years old, Nicolas Cage had been acting for the best part of five years, and his slow-to-develop career was in danger of stalling altogether after the critical drubbing he'd taken over his acting experiments in *Peggy Sue Got Married*. Adrift and without work, Nic once again came close to giving up on acting altogether.

While he had no regrets about the way he'd played his parts, Nic began to believe that his experimental and method-based approach to his diverse roles had brought his career to a premature end. Despite his fears, it was that very performance – so criticised by reviewers – that brought Nic to the attention of both the Coen Brothers and Cher, Hollywood power brokers who would take his career into a whole new phase.

Film-making brothers Joel and Ethan Coen are an unusual and remarkable pair in a number of ways. They've worked together successfully since their debut low-budget *film noir* thriller *Blood Simple* opened to huge critical acclaim but little box office success. Yet, they've kept on going, until in 1997 they finally struck gold with an Oscar for their black comedy-drama *Fargo*.

'They're symbiotic,' said actor Tim Robbins, who worked with the pair on the Joel Silver-produced *The Hudsucker Proxy*. 'They are completely on the same wavelength and will finish each other's sentences. I've never seen them argue.' Both brothers contribute to the scripts of their movies, while Joel directs and Ethan produces. It's an unusual working partnership – both for its longevity and the brothers' refusal to play by the Hollywood rules.

Blood Simple had been an unlikely critical success, with its spin on *film noir*, its black humour and low-budget production values. Stylish and unique, the Coens set out to develop a follow-up. 'We didn't want to do another scary movie,' said Joel of their plans for *Raising Arizona*. 'We'd gotten that out of our system. *Blood Simple* was slow and deliberate. We wanted to try something with a faster pace and a lighter tone. We were ready to do something different.' *Raising Arizona* was to be a frantic farce made in the style of a live-action Roadrunner cartoon about an odd couple who are determined to acquire a baby, no matter what. Filling the lead roles on the project set the pair thinking hard. 'Casting is important – they're the people who have to make the movie work,' noted Joel. 'We knew Holly [Hunter] as a friend, and we'd seen a lot of her work.' Hunter – who had been unavailable for the lead role in *Blood Simple* due to stage commitments – signed on to play policewoman Edwina, infertile but desperate for a child. For Holly Hunter, who had not by then made a great impression in the movies, 1987 was to be her year. As well as *Raising Arizona*, she featured in Volker Schlondorff's *A Gathering Of Old Men, End Of The Line,* and was nominated for an Oscar for *Broadcast News.* She would later win the Best Actress Oscar for her cast-against-type role in *The Piano* and would be nominated again for *The Firm,* both made in 1993.

The Coen Brothers now needed a fearless and versatile actor to play the part of the sympathetic thief and kidnapper H. I. McDonnough. It was a harder part to fill. The character was an odd one – a none-too-clever kooky guy who robs stores and marries Edwina, the policewoman who arrests him. When Joel and Ethan Coen saw *Peggy Sue Got Married,* they knew they had their man. 'Nic was perfect. H. I. is a thinker,' claimed Joel. 'He struggles with grand issues, but he has an urge to hold up convenience stores. He's torn – on the one side is his desire to settle down and have a family, on the other is his inclination to respond to the call of the wild.'

Nic auditioned for the role, but found he didn't win the part automatically, despite the brothers' earlier convictions. *Raising Arizona* is set in the rural heartland of America, and when Nic performed for them, Joel and Ethan began to worry that he was 'too urban' for the role. However, after trying out several other actors, they found they kept returning to him. He had a bizarre cartoony quality which had come across in *Peggy Sue Got Married,* and which they felt would be ideal. He won the part because of, not in spite of, his heavily criticised performances as Charlie Bodell.

Nic was keen to play the part as soon as he'd seen the script. 'What I liked best about this character was his humility,' the actor said about H. I. McDonnough. 'He was a very unusual guy. He played by his own rules, but had a lot of integrity. The first contact I had with the film was through the script, and I was sold as soon as I read it. I was impressed with it because it required no adjustments. It was terrific to finally find one like that.'

The comic tale had Cage's character setting out to kidnap the Arizona quintuplets, heirs to the fortune of furniture tycoon Nathan Arizona. Joel Coen saw the film as 'a love story that lets us examine the question of parenting. It had all the basic elements of contemporary [1987] movie-making – babies, Harley Davidsons and high explosives.'

Working with the Coens was a match made in heaven for Nicolas – they were as irreverent in their approach to the accepted way of movie-making as he was to acting. 'These guys are dangerous,' he claimed. 'They're kind of experimentalists, trying new styles, going to the edge . . . it's very exciting.'

Things didn't get off to a great start for Nic, though, when he arrived on location in Scottsdale, Arizona for the duration of the shoot. He discovered his canvas chair – in which he'd be spending a lot of time waiting around between scene set ups –

Nic's take on H. I. McDonnough in Raising Arizona *was to see the role as a cartoon character brought to life.*

featured a common misspelling of his name. The back of the chair read: 'Nicholas Cage'. Some quick thinking and a trip to the first aid officer and the offending 'h' had been obscured by a strategically placed Band-Aid.

Nic had come to Scottsdale brimming with ideas for his interpretation of the role of H. I. McDonnough. His initial discussions with the Coens had been about the cartoon nature of much of the film, so he planned on playing the role as though he were a cartoon character brought to life. Holly Hunter claimed he based his characterisation on Woody Woodpecker. 'As an actor, Nic is not a people pleaser,' she said of her co-star. 'He's there to please himself. He has a loyalty to his character and a faith in his own ingenuity that a lot of actors don't have, and I really admire that.'

Thinking his own voice was boring – which had been part of the reason for the changes he made in *Peggy Sue Got Married* – Nic set out to commit to celluloid another off-the-wall interpretation. 'I never felt my voice had any character to it on its own merit. So I was always trying to experiment. Sometimes when I'm working on a part I'll actually do the opposite of method acting, I'll read a line in a script and play with it vocally, externally. I'll try to find a melody or a rhythm for it. Then, only after I've got that down will I go behind the line and put in whatever other stuff it needs to make it come to life.'

Nic didn't have much experience with children and when he turned up on the set of *Raising Arizona* he firmly believed that all babies looked alike. After four days struggling with fifteen crawling, drooling babies and ten tough baby wranglers, he'd learned much. 'Yeah, it was kinda chaotic. I had very little experience with babies and there I was with a roomful of them, in the crib, standing by for the crib, waiting to stand by for the crib. They were all guarded by very militant, very watchful stunt mothers. It didn't put me off them for life, but it was tedious when one started crying and we had to stop whatever we were doing until it calmed down.'

It was up to the Coen Brothers to control the maverick talent they'd enlisted to play the central character in the film. As a result of the creative tensions between their desire to end up with a coherent film and Nicolas's desire to indulge his need to toy with his characters, arguments were inevitable. The duo behind the movie and the actor in front of the camera had a lot of respect for each other, but Joel had to keep Nic under his thumb for much of the time. During a supermarket robbery when Nic is running off with a bag of nappies, with a ridiculous-looking stocking over his head, he wanted his character to stop the action for a second, look at his watch, then carry on – just as if he were in a cartoon. 'No,' said Joel, 'not this time. He's a fast and fierce thinker. He's always coming up with new stuff to do – he never takes the obvious choices.'

Nic was excited about the role for the new opportunities it allowed him. 'This was the first time I'd really had the chance to do action,' he recalled. 'There were fight sequences, dog chases. It was the most physically demanding character I'd ever played. Joel listened to the actors and was willing to try things out. That's something about Joel – he'll go with the dangerous.'

Unlike *Peggy Sue Got Married*, Nic's performance was restrained by the director. This time, the balance between outrageous characterisation and directorial responsibility seemed to be just right. 'Joel and Ethan have a very strong vision and I realised how difficult it is for them to accept another artist's vision,' was Nic's way of explaining the fraught working relationship that developed. 'They have an autocratic nature. The important thing is not to discourage an actor's creative flow.'

He had other ideas to contribute to the film. 'I looked at silent films and tried to copy some of the movement,' he said of his influences. 'I would ask to see the storyboards – that way, I could start looking at the camera angles as they were drawn, and I could figure out how to kind of give my body a heightened, almost surreal movement within the frame. And I had this little tooth rigged to come out of my mouth – so when [Tex Cobb] hit me I could spit the tooth in his face. It was the only movie where I ever got that technical.'

Nicolas's love of silent movies also proved to be an inspiration, especially gothic films, like *Dracula*, *Nosferatu* and *The Phantom Of The Opera*. He admired the silent performances of Lon Chaney – who changed his image through skilful make-up for each film – and Max Schreck, who played cinema's first Dracula in *Nosferatu*. 'Because it was silent film, people were overcompensating in terms of gesture and expression,' he noted. 'It seemed to be the one way you could get surreal, like a painter does or a musician does, with acting. How do you do that in modern cinema? The character either has to be insane, drunk, or in a slapstick comedy.'

Another strong influence for him on *Raising Arizona* was Jerry Lewis, whom Jim

Nic used his knowledge of silent cinema to bring a surreal edge to the slapstick comedy of Raising Arizona.

Carrey would also use as a model for many of his acting roles. 'Look at his work in terms of moving pictures,' said Nic of Lewis. 'Turn the sound off and just watch his movements. He's amazing. Lewis made room for people and he's so far out. I met a bunch of comedians who all consider Lewis to be a pioneer of surreal comedy.'

It was the first time that Nic had found his oddball nature could be harnessed by a director to improve the final performance, not allowing him to dominate the film as he had done previously. Improvisation – something else Nic was keen on – was discouraged on *Raising Arizona*, as all the comedy had been carefully worked out in the script. Again, he found it to his advantage to control his natural instincts. 'We were all just trying to make the most of what was on paper,' he said. 'We didn't do a lot of improvisation, because the screenplay was so reliable. Sometimes when you improvise it seems funny, but in the overview it's only distracting.'

The absurdity of *Raising Arizona* was precisely what had attracted Nicolas Cage to the film. 'It was a lot of fun. The movie has an absurd take on life, which is really what I'm into. I like absurd things. Something about absurdity is just loaded with all kinds of wonder. It's ridiculous and unacceptable, but real in its own way, I guess.'

Writing in the *Washington Post*, Rita Kempley was much taken with the new cartoon Cage. '[He] hooks us the minute we lay eyes on him. He's got that blank look that Wile E. Coyote gets after he's been hit between the eyes with an anvil. Nevertheless he is a deep thinker, without the IQ to support his habit. The cartoon look carries over to his hairdo – like Woody Woodpecker's topknot without benefit of styling gel. Cage, who proved himself a fine dramatic actor as the bandaged Vietnam veteran of *Birdy*, brings that same sort of Innocence Lost to this absurd part.

Badly cast as the husband in *Peggy Sue Got Married*, he makes up for that lapse as a loveable loser who can say things like "I cannot tarry" and get away with it.'

Sixties pop star Cher (her real name is Cherilyn Sarkisian) had tried acting in films during that decade – *Good Times* in 1967 and in *Chastity* in 1969 – with very little success. In the seventies, after the break-up of her partnership with Sonny Bono, she stuck to singing, playing lucrative seasons in Las Vegas and hanging on the arms of a succession of men. It wasn't until 1982 that she seriously returned to acting – winning a role in Robert Altman's Broadway production of *Welcome To The Five And Dime Jimmy Dean, Jimmy Dean*. That led to a part in the movie version, and a scene-stealing bit part opposite Meryl Streep in the nuclear drama *Silkwood* in 1983. She went from lesbian punk in *Silkwood* to hippie mom in the 1985 weepy *Mask*, and seemed to be making a success of Hollywood at last. She was difficult to cast, full of attitude and celebrity vibes, but she had the power to affect the outcome of each movie she got involved in.

Like Holly Hunter, Cher would feature in three movies in 1987, and one of them would net her an Oscar. She was one of a trio of spellcasters (alongside Susan Sarandon and Michelle Pfeiffer) faced with Jack Nicholson's devil in *The Witches Of Eastwick*, played a somewhat unlikely lawyer in Peter Yates' dim *Suspect* and played to the gallery in the romantic soap opera/sitcom that was *Moonstruck*.

Cher wielded her power well, often working to strengthen her co-stars, knowing that if she was surrounded by actors of quality or unique talent, it would all reflect back on her central performance. She first saw Nicolas Cage when she was recovering in bed after a car accident and watched *Peggy Sue Got Married*. Far from his performance putting her off from finding out more about this unusual young actor, she immediately decided he'd be ideal as her young suitor in *Moonstruck*.

In the film she was set to play a young widow, Loretta, about to marry steadfast and boring Johnny (Danny Aiello), when she falls for his younger brother, Ronny, a lowly baker who has a wooden hand left hand, having lost the original in an accident with a bread slicer. Cher saw Cage as ideal for the part of Ronny. 'It seemed natural to me. He was Ronny. I didn't see that there could be any problems . . .' She also said of him 'When I think of Nicky, I think of big, blousy, Hamlet-type shirts. I see Nicky as this old-fashioned, gallant type of artist.'

Her proposal horrified *Moonstruck*'s director Norman Jewison and brought the wrath of the studio heads down upon the production. They refused to sanction the casting of Nicolas Cage, the guy with the wacky voice and bizarre attitude from *Peggy Sue Got Married*. They were determined he was not going to unbalance *Moonstruck* the way he had Coppola's film. However, Cher was equally determined that Nic was the guy for her, and she promptly went on strike for 24 hours, refusing to continue with the film until Nic was secured for the role. According to Norman Jewison, 'the main reason she thought he was right for the part was because, like the character of Ronny, Nicolas struck her as a tormented soul'.

'Cher was a real champion for me,' said a grateful Nic, even if he wasn't that enamoured with the film to begin with. 'I didn't want to do the movie at first. I wanted to do some punk movie, some wild, rebellious gesture. It's only now that I look back and realise how lucky I was. I don't think I was mature enough to know it or to tell anybody at the time. The film was my first blockbuster.'

To provide some kind of insurance, Jewison and the studio heads from MGM insisted that Nic do a screen test for the movie, showing the approach he was intending to take to the part. 'They wanted to make sure that I wasn't going to turn the part into something that wasn't on the page.'

Once he agreed to the role, 23-year-old Cage remembered he used to watch the now 42-year-old Cher on TV back in his childhood on *The Sonny And Cher Show*. He had been particularly fascinated by Sonny Bono's moustache, which had created a desire in young Nicolas to grow one himself – something he hasn't yet done. Now, he was about to play Cher's lover, an offbeat young Italian-American baker who was to sweep the somewhat frumpy Jewish widow off her feet.

The casting of Nic was just the latest in a series of set-backs that director Norman Jewison had suffered. He hadn't intended to make *Moonstruck* at all, signing up with MGM to develop a remake of the 1937 film *The Man Who Could Work Miracles*, based on a novel by H. G. Wells. As the director of *In The Heat Of The Night, Fiddler On The Roof*, and *Jesus Christ Superstar*, Jewison had made a variety of films, but had never had a huge hit. When his H. G. Wells movie stalled at MGM, they offered him the script

Nic as the young Italian-American baker who sweeps Cher's Jewish widow off her feet in Moonstruck. *'The film was my first blockbuster,' he later said.*

of *Moonstruck* in compensation. 'It came in with the title *The Bridge And The Wolf*, and a lot of people thought it was a horror movie. After all the frustration, I was in the mood for a romantic comedy, and I identified with the betrayals in the family.'

Working with a veteran like Jewison was a very different experience for Nicolas from working with the young mavericks Joel and Ethan Coen, who were much more on his own weird wavelength: 'It was a real shift in gear after doing comedy with the Coens. It's not experimental like with them. Norman's got 30 years experience, knows what he wants and has developed his style. It's good in a different way. With Norman it's like being in an armoured car – you know you'll get there safely and he'll provide good work.'

Compared with some other directors he'd worked with, Nic found Jewison to be an actor's director rather than one who was more concerned with the placing of his camera and the integration of special effects. 'He likes actors and has evolved a style that leans on them. His work is starting to get simpler. He told me he used to play with the camera – all that split-screen stuff in *The Thomas Crown Affair*, for example – but now he wants to concentrate on the people. He works closer with actors than [Alan] Parker or [Francis Ford] Coppola.'

So it was that Jewison found himself choreographing the comings and goings of the Castorini clan. Seven years after being widowed and keen to have a child, Cher's downbeat, cardigan-clad Loretta commits to Aiello's Johnny Cammareri as an act of final desperation. He's a stick-in-the-mud, not at all adventurous and romantic – but Loretta could be waiting forever to meet someone with those qualities. It's only when Johnny jets off to Palermo in Italy to attend the bedside of his dying mother, and she tracks down Johnny's younger brother, Ronny, that Loretta discovers Mr Right: during a period of full moon, he transforms from a sweaty, beast-like bakery worker to a hopelessly romantic, James Stewart-like opera-loving leading man. It was a character that got Nic's creative juices flowing as he conjured up one of his off-the-wall interpretations, a take on the part that was to bring him into conflict with Jewison.

Nic decided he'd play Ronny as the creature from one of his favourite movies, Cocteau's *Beauty And The Beast*. He saw in the character a beast-like side, reflected in the 'wolf' element of the script's original title, that he wanted to bring to the fore. 'I didn't change my character from the way it was written, but I did try to play up the wolfish part of Ronny's personality.' Unfortunately, Norman Jewison was not in accord with his leading man and Nic found himself on the verge of being fired from a movie once again.

'Nicolas did have a darker interpretation of Ronny than I did,' confirmed Jewison. 'We both agreed that a poetic quality was central to the character. When Ronny is first introduced in the film he's in a basement slaving over hot ovens and he almost has the quality of a young Lord Byron. As the film progresses, Nicolas blossoms into a classic romantic leading man. I think it was the first film where he'd come off that way. He had the gangling, vulnerable appeal of a young Jimmy Stewart.' It was an approach that Cage would develop more fully during his comedy trio of *Honeymoon In Vegas, It Could Happen To You* and *Guarding Tess*.

Jewison tried, as had the Coen Brothers, to control his leading man, to contain his

During the full moon Nic's Ronny transforms from a beast-like bakery worker into an opera-loving romantic.

excesses to the benefit of the film. 'He took unbelievable chances as an actor,' Jewison said. 'Every time I got angry with him I'd just look in his eyes. In fact, I don't think I saw any other part of Nicky except his eyes. He was a gambler.' Cage's friend Jim Carrey had seen this before on *Peggy Sue Got Married.* 'Nic is a representative of the Picasso form of acting,' suggested Carrey. 'He doesn't mind putting the two eyes on one side of the face.'

The tensions sometimes erupted on the set, and Nic returned to his habits of *The Cotton Club* as a way of coping – he screamed at the top of his lungs and threw a chair across the soundstage to release some of the frustration he was suffering as Jewison attempted more and more to hem in and tone down his approach. Nic has confessed: 'I was still borrowing from the more heightened gestures of the silent movie days. If you look at *Metropolis,* there's a shot of the scientist who invents the technology to create the robot woman – he shows off the robot hand that he invented. He has it raised up, and I told Norman [Jewison] that I really wanted to approximate that shot. He thought it was nuts, but he went for it – so I could pull the glove off and show the wooden hand.'

Like Coppola on *Peggy Sue Got Married,* Jewison had his cast take part in two weeks' rehearsal before shooting started in December 1986 at the Casa Italian Bakery on Ninth Avenue in New York. Location work took Nic around the city, from Little Italy to Greenwich Village and to a house in Brooklyn Heights used as the frontage for Cher's family home. The scene which takes place at the Metropolitan Opera

59

involved 300 extras working over six hours who mingled with real audiences attending shows at the Lincoln Center. The rest of the opera interiors – and much of the rest of the film – were shot in Toronto, with the Markham Theatre standing in for the interior of the Lincoln Centre. Post-production also took place in Toronto and production wrapped the day before Valentine's Day on Friday 13 February 1987 – the day of a full moon.

The critics took well to *Moonstruck*. Roger Ebert, writing in the *Chicago Sun-Times*, was impressed by the acting: 'The movie is filled with fine performances – by Cher, never funnier or more assured, and by Cage as the hapless, angry brother, who is so filled with hurts that he has lost track of what caused them. In its warmth and in its enchantment, as well as in its laughs, this is the best comedy in a long time.' On the film's January 1988 release the *Washington Post* agreed with Rita Kempley, noting of Cage and Cher: 'They're an irresistibly offbeat couple – Cage playing on the edge, where he likes it; Cher creating a fairy-tale realist, captivating yet cautious. He looks like the bastard son of Mama Celeste and Wile E. Coyote, and she, as the camera romances her Mediterranean features, is Mona Lisa in heavy mascara.'

The double whammy of *Raising Arizona* and *Moonstruck* had launched Nicolas Cage as a quirky and strangely charming Everyman. But while he was enjoying the first flushes of success on the big screen, Nic's personal life was in turmoil.

His on and off relationship with actress Jenny Wright was finally disintegrating

The Washington Post *dubbed Nic and Cher 'an irrestistably offbeat couple'.*

as the pair drifted apart. Her career seemed to have stalled – and as Nic began work on *Moonstruck*, her constant unfounded insecurity about his potential liaisons with his female co-stars took their toll. The pair agreed to split up – but Nic was the one who found himself going to pieces when the romance died.

'I cry a lot,' he admitted. 'My emotions are very close to the surface. I don't want to hold anything in so it festers and turns into pus – a pustule of emotion that explodes into a festering cesspool of depression.' Ever resourceful, he found a way to use his emotional turmoil in the part he was playing in *Moonstruck*. Ronny was supposed to be pouring his heart out in romantic pleadings to Cher's Loretta. Instead, Nic imagined he was sending messages to Jenny Wright. 'I was kind of hoping that Jenny would be out there somewhere to hear my romantic pleading,' he reluctantly admitted. In fact, Nic came to fear that getting the attention of Jenny Wright had been his main reason for taking the role opposite Cher. 'I wanted her to see me as a handsome motherfucker in a tuxedo looking at a beautiful woman and also saying it's OK to be in love and to be screwed up, 'cos love rules. It's complex. I wanted to show her the messiness of love and I wanted her to be turned on by how handsome I was. She wasn't. I wanted us to start again. We didn't. So, I gotta question that particular role.'

Perhaps there were further consolations for Nic on the set of *Moonstruck*, as the production was swept with rumours that he and Cher were engaged in a passionate and violent affair. The stories were not as bizarre as they might have seemed. Cher was well known for her casual flings with younger men, following her abortive marriages to Sonny Bono and rock guitarist Greg Allman. One of her boyfriends, 24-year-old Rob Camiletti, had been charged with attempting to run down a photographer who was trying to snatch illicit shots of the pair. At 23, Cage was just the right age.

Movie stars in Cher's romantic hit list already included Tom Cruise and Val Kilmer, who later played the rubber-clad Batman in *Batman Forever*. Asked directly about the rumours of a wild tryst with Cher, Nic neither confirmed nor denied the tales. 'She's a passionate woman,' he said of her. He was very concerned with making his love scenes with her in the film seem realistic. 'I didn't want to kiss her until the time I had to kiss her in the film. It really worked, it was exciting.'

Whatever the truth of their romantic liaisons off-screen, Cher developed worries about being upstaged by her co-star on screen. Nic was taken out to dinner by Norman Jewison after shooting and told that his role in the film was to be reduced. 'Some of my best work was cut out by the director,' Nic lamented. 'He said he had to cut some of the scenes because they overshadowed the star.' Whether Cher's influence had continued into the editing of the film, or Jewison was using her powerful position as a cover for his own desire to cut away at Nic's part, his role in *Moonstruck* was certainly reduced from what it had been in the original script.

Freed from the film and freed from his romance with Jenny Wright, Nicolas returned to his drinking and brawling ways in Los Angeles – but this time he was a movie star with money to spend. Now he was a bona fide Hollywood bachelor and he set out to compensate for his nerdy adolescence. He would spend time with Johnny Depp – now on his way to becoming a movie star too – and Jim Carrey – who was still toiling away in big-screen bit parts and TV shows. Julian Lennon, the son of John Lennon, was also a drinking pal (he later turned up in *Leaving Las Vegas*), as was Nic's erstwhile co-star Sean Penn, who was drowning his own romantic sorrows after breaking up with Madonna.

Having split from Jenny Wright, Nic decided he'd had enough of living in seedy apartments around Hollywood and would invest some of his movie money in property. He decided in 1988 he would go house-hunting and 'get myself a place'. The place he chose was unusual – a fake gothic castle on a third of an acre in Loz Feliz, in the heart of the Hollywood Hills. The list price of the gaudy building – complete with turrets, battlements and a series of challenging staircases – was $1,695,000. Negotiating with representatives of Douglas Properties who were handling the 1928 building, he got the price down to $1.5 million. The building, which had been entirely refurbished only two years previously in 1986, boasted three bathrooms, four bedrooms and quarters for a live-in maid. The route to the front door of the white stucco-clad castle is up a long, twisting white staircase, illuminated either side by little white lights. Nic has said that he hates the stucco, and hopes one day to buy a real castle rather than this faked-up one, maybe even importing one brick-by-brick from Europe and rebuilding it in Los Angeles.

The money he'd earned from his most recent movies allowed him to decorate the house thoroughly, indulging in what he termed his 'hot rod gothic' decor. The living room boasts a panoramic view of Los Angeles and a black marble fireplace as a centrepiece. A plush velvet sofa dominates the room, looked down upon by a Robert Williams painting of Somay, a Hindu goddess. Over the fireplace hangs a 6ft metal fly. Elsewhere in this den suitable for Dracula are carved gargoyles, a pinned butterfly collection held under glass, and a stuffed black beetle from the spooky sixties TV series *The Outer Limits*. It was a prop that Nic 'just had to have'.

Having failed to bring inspiration from Cocteau's *Beauty And The Beast* to bear on *Moonstruck*, he indulged it at home. 'It's the sort of feeling I've admired since I saw Jean Cocteau's [film]. That was my dream as a child – to live in the Beast's castle.' Finally earning big sums as an actor, Nic was happy to indulge himself and achieve some of his childhood dreams. Having money to spend was not going to be something he would ever be embarrassed about. 'These actors work all their lives and start to make money and say: "I'm not really into it, the money's no big deal." I think of the guy who's out there struggling for his next dime, listening to the actor saying his millions are no big deal . . .'

In some ways, Nic had achieved his ambitions in only seven years. He'd set out to achieve the same kind of wealth and security through acting that his Uncle Francis had gained from directing. Jealousy and the desire for fame and fortune had been the original driving forces of his ambitions. Now he'd arrived – and he had to find another motivation to continue with his acting career.

Nic has always been upfront about his enjoyment of sex. It was one of the motivations in becoming an actor. 'You have to remember I started acting when I was seventeen and the hormones were going crazy. I assumed that if I was an actor I would meet more girls. And I did – and I paid for it. I thought that someone was interested in me and didn't want to admit that it was something else.' On the rebound from his relationship with Jenny Wright, he had embarked on what he once dubbed his 'bacchanalian era' – and the pursuit of sex was central.

Despite enjoying the chase, Nic came to regard the act itself as rather odd. 'If you're smart and you think about it, sex can be considered ridiculous,' he claimed. 'If you really look at the act of what we're doing, it's crazy, and the only way that I'm able to rationalise it is that it's instinct, it's totally out of our control and it's symbolic of some kind of creation. But if you look at it, just the physical thing of doing it, it's absolutely ridiculous.'

Perhaps Cage spent too long thinking about sex because he was about to meet a woman who would have a remarkable effect on him. 'I agree that sex is super-important, but I can remember eight years ago being so in love with a person and not being able to have sex, because I was paralysed. I couldn't perform on that level. And I married her later.'

The strange tale of the courtship between Nicolas Cage and Patricia Arquette is like a bizarre plot from one of Nic's offbeat films. When the couple first met in 1987, Patricia was nineteen and just setting out on an acting career with a featured role in *A Nightmare On Elm Street Part 3: Dream Warriors*, whereas Nic was 23 and had just become a comic leading man thanks to *Raising Arizona* and *Moonstruck*.

Like Nic's, Patricia's family had a background in the film business. She was part of the fourth generation of the Arquettes to be entertainers. Her great-grandparents had been big on the vaudeville circuit, while her grandfather Cliff Arquette featured on the long-running game show *Hollywood Squares*, under the name Charley Weaver. Her father Lewis Arquette had played in starring roles on Broadway. Her older sister Rosanna Arquette was better known in the late eighties for her kooky roles in *Desperately Seeking Susan*, Martin Scorsese's *After Hours* and *Silverado*. Years later her brother David would join the acting clan when he featured as the comic dumb sheriff in Wes Craven's ironic horror hit *Scream*. Patricia's other two brothers, Richard and Alexis are also actors – though they haven't had the successes yet of the other three.

Acting hadn't come easy to the younger Arquette sister. 'When I told Rosanna I wanted to be an actress, I was really afraid about it as she was doing so well,' she recalled. 'I was going through a really insecure time in my life, but she said, "Look, I really believe in you. I know you can do it."' Patricia had started acting young, but it was her battle with dream demon Freddy Krueger in 1987's *Dream Warriors* that first brought her to mainstream attention. Nevertheless, when offered a role in the next Freddy frightfest, she declined. 'I was very honoured, but I didn't want to get stuck doing horror for the rest of my life.'

Canter's Deli in Los Angeles is a hip eatery with a young and affluent clientele, many of them rising stars in Hollywood. It had been a hang-out of Nic's for a while, and it was here in 1987 that he first met Patricia. 'She walked passed me and she'd just eaten liver and onions. I fell in love with her there and then. I said: "Listen, you don't believe me but I want to marry you!" She said no. I said: "Put me on a quest. Let me prove how much I mean this." And so she went back to her table and she wrote this list down on a napkin of things she wanted.'

Patricia had been taken aback by Nic's out-of-the-blue proposal. 'The second thing he said to me was "I'm going to marry you!",' she remembers. She tried to laugh off the approach, but when Nic insisted on the list for his quest, she acquiesced – if that's what it took to get rid of the guy.

The idea of the grand romantic quest for a series of impossible objects appealed to Nic's off-kilter imagination. 'I've always been a victim of the over-the-top grand romantic gesture,' he admitted to *Premiere* magazine. 'I've made a romantic fool of myself many, many times, by performing grand gestures when I'm not wanted.' To begin with, certainly, he wasn't wanted by Patricia and she concocted a list calculated to be impossible to complete. Top of it was the autograph of notorious recluse J. D. Salinger, author of *The Catcher In The Rye*. Next came a black orchid, followed by a wedding dress from the Lisu tribe in South East Asia, and one of the chained-down, fibreglass statues from a Big Bob hamburger joint. She expected Nic to concede defeat and slink away, but he was impervious to the irony evident in her requests.

Picking on what he thought would be the easiest to get hold of, Nic zoomed off on his Harley motorbike to a flower store in search of a black orchid. '"Can I have a black orchid, please?",' he recalls naively asking. 'And they said: "There's no such thing as a black orchid!" I knew something was askew. So, I said: "Gimme the purple orchid." I took that and went to the art store and got some black paint.'

Patricia thought she'd seen the last of the weird guy who'd pestered her at Canter's Deli – until he turned up on her doorstep. 'I hear this motorcycle outside my mother's house,' she recalled later. 'I peek out the window and there he is with a purple orchid and a black spray paint can and he's spraying it!'

Nic then set out in search of a J. D. Salinger autograph, despite his manager Gerry Harrington – who was friends with Salinger's son – pointing out that the mysterious author had deliberately not signed anything that was publicly available. Nic's movie cash came in handy on this part of the mission. 'I found one at a place on Beverly Boulevard. It was a hand-written letter and it cost a lot of money – \$2,500.' Nic paid happily, and prepared to deliver it to Arquette, despite others' fears about the signature's authenticity. 'A lot of people don't believe it,' admitted Cage, 'because they know that J. D. Salinger never signed anything. But this was a letter he wrote, so I bought it. I had it.'

Patricia received another visit. This time she was in the street, according to Nic, playing hopscotch. He'd packaged the letter up in a cigar box and he dropped it off at her house, disappearing just before she found it. Patricia was amazed and surprised by the lengths Nic was going to, and decided she'd better give him a second look. 'Every day a new thing would show up at my door,' she said of his lunatic attempts to romance her. 'The deal was when he'd finished I had to marry him. I had never even gone on a date with him! I said, "OK, OK! Stop! I'll go on a

Nic began to date model/actress Christine Fulton after his quest to win the hand of Patricia Arquette failed.

date." It was very fairy tale like. We met as two kids who fall in love.'

Nic was delighted that his pigheaded stubbornness had won out, but he discovered that his ardour for Arquette was so great he was afraid of getting onto a sexual relationship with the woman he had loved from afar. 'I remember being so in love I wasn't able to have sex because I was paralysed.' The pair embarked on a vacation trip to Mexico, but the holiday where Nic hoped he'd be able to relax and the relationship could progress turned into a nightmare.

After a stay in Mexico City, the pair decided to fly to Cuba, where Nic's grandfather Carmine Coppola was conducting *Napoleon*. Cage had a bizarre idea at the back of his mind – he would abduct Patricia while in Cuba and make her marry him. They didn't get further than the airport, though, when a mix-up over the tickets resulted in Nic throwing the kind of temper tantrum he usually restricted to movie sets. As a result the pair were not allowed on the plane, and Patricia had seen a new and disturbing side of Nicolas Cage. They stayed in Mexico a short while longer, bumming around and checking out gigs, before returning to Los Angeles.

Patricia felt she'd given Nic enough time and attention after the madness of his bizarre courtship. She backed off from seeing him again when they got back to Los Angeles and resumed her relationship with her boyfriend, Paul Rossi, a video company owner and musician who was in a band called Wasted Youth. She had a big audition coming up for the lead part in a film based on Hubert Selby Jr's *Last Exit To Brooklyn* and didn't want additional distractions. She tried out for the film in New York, then returned to Los Angeles to discover something of a shock. She was pregnant – at age nineteen – the father being Paul Rossi. The pair discussed their situation, and although Rossi made it clear he didn't want to get married, he would take part in the raising of the child if she had it. She decided she would. Then the word came through that she was wanted for the role of the hooker on *Last Exit To Brooklyn*. It was a tricky situation. The film required her to play a rape scene and to stay unnaturally thin as her character was a drug addict. It wasn't compatible with having a child, so Patricia turned down the role, which went to Jennifer Jason Leigh. Instead, she had her son, Enzo – named after a minor character in Francis Ford Coppola's *The Godfather*.

Nic was devastated that his passion for Patricia hadn't gone past first base. She had several reasons for calling things off with him – primarily, there were her already complicated life and her youth. She also felt her movie career to date was nowhere near as successful as his – a factor she knew had been a problem for Nicolas and Wright previously. 'I felt unworthy of him in a way,' she lamented of the period when the first flush of their bizarre romance cooled. 'He was already doing things in his life, and I felt that if I was with him, this love I had for him, I would never be anything on my own. I would just become invisible – not to the world, but to myself. I had the idea that I had to go through a lot of shit to grow up, and that there would be blood let on both sides. I didn't want that scar tissue between us. I said, "We're not mature enough to handle something so amazing as this, so let's walk away now, because I refuse to damage this."'

Nic and Patricia decided just to be friends, and she never got her fibreglass statue from Big Bob's or the wedding dress from the tribe in Asia. They would talk on the phone – often with long gaps of months in between – and Nic would periodically ask her to marry him. She'd try to put him off, using Enzo and Paul Rossi as an excuse. On his own again, Nic threw himself into the two things he always fell back on – work and women.

He became even more of a dating machine than he'd been between going out with Wright and Arquette. A string of one-night stands and brief flings filled his time and served to put his failure with Patricia behind him. There were problems, though, with the kind of women he was meeting. 'Living life as an actor, it's hard not to hurt people. There is a distance in relationships,' he admitted. 'You're away a lot and it's hard not to hurt or be hurt. I've only met actresses and models, and there's been an instability there.'

Despite being aware of these problems, Nicolas's next 'unstable' relationship was with a model named Christina (sometimes Kristina) Fulton. She was what has become know in Hollywood as a Model-Actress-Whatever, a figure who hangs around on the fringes of the film business, does modelling assignments, perhaps wins bit parts in movies, but doesn't get the big break needed to become a star. Her biggest claim to fame was the 1991 Oliver Stone film *The Doors* where she plays one of the Jim Morrison groupies, and is featured making love to Val Kilmer's Morrison in a lift.

Nic was smitten and Christina moved in with him. Both were aware of the pitfalls of this kind of relationship where they would often be apart, but even with this recognition it was to take its toll. Despite his involvement with Christina, Nic was still pining for Patricia. She'd begun to return his occasional phone calls, mischievously asking him, 'Do you still want to marry me?' Nic's response to these confusing romantic troubles was to find relief in work. He was an established leading man now after *Moonstruck* – he could surely find a decent role to continue to build on his new found fame, wealth and success? That might have been the approach of any 'ordinary' actor, but Nic was far from ordinary and was not in the frame of mind to look at his next role as another rung on the career ladder. Instead, he indulged himself once more, committing to the leading role in the downright weird *Vampire's Kiss*. In it he was to play a New York literary editor who comes to believe he's turning into a vampire. It was not the kind of step that would bring Nic any nearer to an Oscar nomination.

5. Wild at Heart & Weird on Top

'I'M SOMETIMES FASCINATED BY WHAT people expect me to be like,' Nicolas Cage admitted in a 1993 interview. 'It's hard for me to understand that if you play a far-out character and you really commit to it, people can't see past the snakeskin jacket [which he wore in *Wild At Heart*] or wooden hand [in *Moonstruck*] and you have to wonder, does anybody remember there's such a thing as acting? I mean, this isn't me! I don't go home with plastic fangs in my mouth. I'm just attracted to these characters simply because they're loaded with interesting behaviour.'

Vampire's Kiss wasn't a true horror movie. The screenplay, by Joseph Minion, was a parody of modern urban life, using the lifestyle of the nocturnal, bloodsucking vampire to skewer the eighties yuppie culture. Nicolas himself was living almost like a vampire at the time. He wasn't getting on with people and liked spending time away from Christina Fulton by retreating to the two bedroom apartment in Hancock Park that he kept on after buying the house in the Hollywood Hills. The area was well known as a retreat for old Hollywood – George Raft had stayed there and it had been alleged that Bing Crosby had once used Nic's building as an illicit lovenest. Nic was staying out all night – rising at around noon and only returning to the building at four or five the following morning. He would take solace in the art with which he covered the walls of his apartment. Nic claimed his Chagall lithograph proudly displayed there had not been purchased 'for the sake of investment' but simply because he 'likes the distraction that good art provides'.

With this kind of routine going on, the chance to play a yuppie who begins acting like one of the undead was irresistible. 'It was the movie nobody wanted me to do,' Nic claimed, 'particularly my agent and my lawyer. I make my own decisions, but it was hard because everybody said don't do it.'

Nic decided he would do it – but then had cold feet as the commercial and professional implications of the film sank in. He pulled out, his agent and lawyer having got the better of him. The film trundled on, and Judd Nelson was cast instead of him. When Nelson bailed out, Dennis Quaid signed up, only to have second thoughts and call it a day too. By now, Nic was regretting his original decision not to make the movie and he didn't want to miss what amounted to a second chance. 'After *Moonstruck*, I thought: OK, now I'm gonna do the movie I care about, *Vampire's Kiss*, this angry, little avant-garde movie. Finally, I went back in, because otherwise I'd feel like a coward. It was important for me to take the chance. It was a great screenplay which just grabbed me by the collar and screamed, "If you don't do this movie you're a fucking coward!" I figure that in order to succeed in the film business, you can't be afraid to roll the dice.'

The producer of *Vampire's Kiss* was Barry Shils, and he knew Nic was the leading man the production needed. 'Nic goes out on a limb and we needed that kind of boldness. There wasn't a lot of money involved, but Nic didn't care. He has guts and he likes to gamble.'

There was another, weird *Twilight Zone* reason for Nic to commit to the film. His ruthless, nasty literary agent character was to be called Peter Loew. Since purchasing his castle in the Hollywood Hills, Nic had been receiving mail addressed to the previous tenant, one Peter Laslow. As far as Nic was concerned, the names were too similar for it not to be an omen, but he didn't want to examine the co-incidence too closely. 'That's another one of those little tears in the envelope of space and time that I don't know how to deal with, and I'm not going to address too much,' he admitted.

Vampire's Kiss seemed like the right movie at the right time, and Cage couldn't resist. 'It's the kind of movie I think has an interesting after-taste,' he noted. 'It stays with you. It's a comedy, a black comedy, but the end of the movie does sort of hit you over the head. It's not a very appealing view of America, and it's not really a movie that can or should be analysed. I think it's the kind of movie that should just be felt, like a bad dream or a scary painting. People either hate it or absolutely love it – both points of view are valid.'

Prior to beginning work on *Vampire's Kiss*, Nic hadn't worked in over a year, despite the success of *Moonstruck*. 'I don't know what happened,' he claimed. 'I felt like, "This is what I'm supposed to do, to work. This is what I want to do." It's very hard as an actor to sit around and wait to be selected, because I start to vegetate. I don't have enough discipline or energy to expose myself to books or enough creative stimulus to get turned on by everyday life, which is really something I should learn to do more often, I think. Go to museums and feel things from a painting.'

As he had done on *Peggy Sue Got Married* and had tried to do on his last two films, Nic set out to make the *Vampire's Kiss* project uniquely his. Its British director Robert Bierman (later to make *Keep The Aspidistra Flying*), was making his first cinema film and was clearly unable to control Nic's more extreme urges. The film has Nic playing a Manhattan literary agent who treats the women around him in the most appalling manner, from his weary secretary (Maria Conchita Alonso) to his therapist (Elizabeth Ashley). Indulging in a series of casual and callous one night stands, Nic's Peter Loew gets involved with Rachel, played by Jennifer Beals. After he is bitten by Rachel during their love-making, Loew comes to the conclusion that she is a vampire – and that he's now well on his way to becoming one. In fact, the succubus character of Rachel may simply be a figment of Loew's deranged imagination as he succumbs to a nervous breakdown.

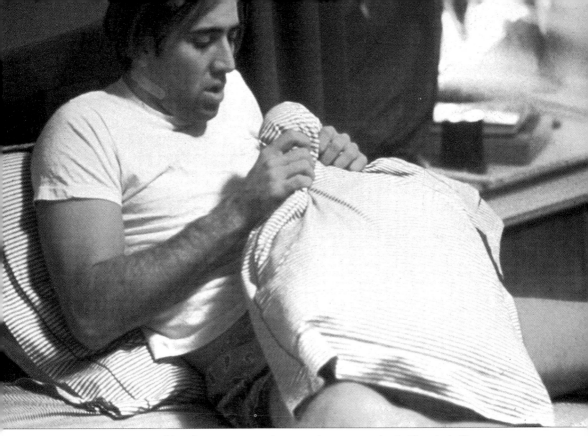

Nic as Peter Loew, a ruthless literary agent who turns into a vampire in Vampire's Kiss.

As Loew's behaviour becomes ever more extreme, from keeping out of the light, avoiding crosses, eating bugs, wearing plastic fangs and skulking about like someone from an old horror movie, his staff and associates pretend not to notice, indulging his extremes as if it were normal behaviour for a literary agent. Nic had a ball with the part. It allowed him to return to the kind of wildness he brought to *Peggy Sue Got Married* – and this time there wasn't a director with the strength of character of Francis Ford Coppola, the Coen Brothers or Norman Jewison to attempt to reign him in. He changed his voice again and played around with different ways of walking. Eventually he settled on a kind of Katherine Hepburn, Philadelphia drawl for the voice. 'Because Peter Loew was hiding behind this absurd facade of intellect, his voice was this *faux*, bogus continental bullshit accent, this pseudo literary English garbage that I've heard people do,' he said. The voice wasn't the end of the transformation Nic was to undergo for the role. In the film Peter Loew watches *Nosferatu*, one of Nic's own favourite films, to find out about vampires. 'The references to Max Schreck are pretty obvious,' Nic admitted of the model for much of his character. 'I was exposed at an early age to silent movies like *Nosferatu, The Cabinet Of Dr Caligari*. They made a big impression on me, they haunted me for years and I was becoming interested in incorporating those gestures into a modern film.'

Nic had partially succeeded in this mission before, when he managed to persuade Norman Jewison to include his homage to Fritz Lang's *Metropolis* in

Moonstruck. Now he was to go much further in *Vampire's Kiss.* 'I thought here was an opportunity to realise some of my expressionistic dreams, or nightmares, because not only was he [Loew] mad, he was crazy thinking he was turning into a vampire. So, I thought it was the perfect way to go. Ultimately, I wanted him to turn into Max Schreck [the actor who played the vampire in *Nosferatu*] with the gestures and the silent film acting style. I don't really see this as a vampire movie, per se. I see it more as a black comedy about a man who is going out of his mind because of a lack of love – loneliness being the reason.'

However, Nic didn't get things all his own way, and producer Barry Shils found he had to take an active part with director Robert Bierman in the fruitless attempt to contain some of their leading man's eccentricities. 'At one point he wanted us to replace the mechanical bat we were using with a real one,' Shils revealed. 'He was worried that the toy one was flying too slowly and audiences would know it was a fake. We told him a real bat was out of the question – it was illegal. They carry rabies and he could be bitten. Nic said it didn't matter, he wanted it to look authentic. He tried to get us to get someone to go out into Central Park in New York and capture one.'

Nic lost that fight, but he was to win one that was much more significant and central to the audience reaction to the movie. Despite a fear of bugs that derived from his childhood nightmares about his mother becoming a beetle, Nic decided he would eat live cockroaches where the screenplay called for his character to swallow raw eggs. Nic had clearly seen the original 1931 Bela Lugosi-starring version of *Dracula* in which Dracula's henchman Renfield had run around the castle catching and eating live insects. 'It was awful,' Nic revealed of his method-acting commitment to making the scene look realistic – by really eating the beasties. 'I couldn't really taste it, but psychologically it was murder. I didn't eat anything for three days. I had difficulty sleeping. I rinsed my mouth out with 100 per cent proof vodka before and after. It was a nightmare.'

Nightmare it may have been, but the sequence, which was to become central to the barmy mythology of Nicolas Cage, was certainly effective when the film was seen. 'I wanted there to be a moment of something so real,' Nic said. 'When I saw the film with an audience, the reaction was so intense. All I had done was eat a cockroach. To this day, people ask me about the cockroach. I actually have a fear of bugs, and it makes me sick thinking about it. I knew doing that was like saving the movie $2 million on special effects. All I had to do was eat a bug, and when you go to the theatre, it's the same reaction – "Oh, no!" I know the reason that movie is still in video stores is partly because of that.'

After the cast and crew screening of the movie, Nic was pleased with himself. 'It was the first film I did that I felt totally satisfied with after seeing. It wasn't an easy process making that film.' However, the later video release was to give Nic serious cause for complaint, The marketing of the film featured a cover shot of him, plastic fangs in place and vampire-style cape hanging from his shoulders. 'I never once wore a cape in the movie. Big business marketed it as some schlock vampire movie, some supernatural piece of shit! For a while there I felt like I couldn't win. I pour my heart and soul into this and then they put me into that stupid cape. What have I gotta do? When that video came out, it really hurt me.'

It wasn't an easy process watching it, either, according to many critics. Hal Hinson writing in the *Washington Post* was astonished at Nic's performance: '*Vampire's Kiss* is a one-of-a-kind movie. As yuppies go, Peter is one of the stranger ones, particularly as Nicolas Cage plays him. *Vampire's Kiss* is stone-dead bad, incoherently bad, but it goes all the way with its premise. You've heard of actors making a strong choice and going with it? Well, see it in the flesh! Stomping, snorting, his hair hanging over his eyes like a curtain of foppish dementia, Cage acts as if he has been taking hits off of Dennis Hopper's gas mask. There's no way to overstate it: This is scorched-earth acting – the most flagrant scenery chewing I've ever seen. Part Dwight Frye in *Dracula*, part Tasmanian devil, Cage makes the previous champ – Crispin Glover in *River's Edge* – look like Perry Como. Cage makes sure that we're never bored, though. No amount of description can prepare you for these mad excesses. They have to be seen to be believed.' Audiences seemed to agree, and the film only took a meagre $725,000 at the US box office.

However, there were some who appreciated the offbeat nature of *Vampire's Kiss* and positively championed Nic's performance, including the queen of American film critics, Pauline Kael, who wrote: 'Cage is airily amazing. He does some of the way out stuff that you love actors in silent movies for doing and he makes it work with sound. This daring kid starts over the top and just keeps going.' *MovieLine* magazine included Nic's film in their Ten Best Performances From An Actor Under 30, and called him cinema's 'designated madman'.

For Terence Rafferty in the *New Yorker*, the appeal of the film lay with Nic's ability to bring out the subtext of the script in his manner of playing. 'Cage delivers a remarkable portrait of a completely obnoxious jerk. He carries everything with a manic intensity that plays with a throwaway ease, but must have required the utmost energy and concentration – not to mention spontaneity. For the first half hour, *Vampire's Kiss* seems to be a total catastrophe. Cage plays his character insanely over the top from nearly the first scene. It becomes clear that the humour and the lack of moderation is wholly intentional. This is basically Cage's show all the way. For pure weirdness, *Vampire's Kiss* is without rival. It's also the most interesting film of the year.'

Nic was prepared for his heartfelt film to fail, despite the mixed reviews. 'When it came out, the public didn't know how to read it,' he explained. 'You can't classify that movie. Is it a real vampire story or just a guy that's going crazy? All great pieces of work are open to interpretation – and this is a great piece of work, of that I'm sure. It's the most adventurous I've ever been in a film. I think time will treat it well.' A screening at the 1990 London Film Festival did give the film a sheen of respectability.

Maintaining his determination to outsmart his critics and continue to go along in his own weird and wonderful way, Nic next made a couple of movies almost no-one was going to see. Far from being driven by commercial criteria, he was out to indulge himself, to push his bizarre talents to the extreme – and if that meant no-one saw the movies or his performances were slated for being 'bad', he just didn't care. 'When I act, I act for myself,' he gleefully and selfishly confirmed. 'I don't worry what they [the critics] think. If they get it, it's great, but if they don't, that's okay too. But if they do respond in a bad way, even that, with *Vampire's Kiss*, means we were able to strike a chord in them, they were affected by it. And that's cool. The worst thing is to be boring or mediocre. I think that's worse than being bad. At least you can talk about it if it's bad.'

In his continuing quest to avoid the boring and mediocre, Nic next agreed to appear in an ultra-low-budget horror flick called *Never On A Tuesday*, directed by newcomer Adam Rifkin. He appears uncredited in the zombie film which starred Claudia Christian – later to win fame as one of the leads on the *Babylon 5* TV series – as the title character, named Tuesday, and Peter Berg, who was later to be the hapless object of attention for Linda Fiorentino's con artist *femme fatale* in *The Last Seduction*. Nic featured in the film as the 'man in the red sports car' and he wasn't alone amongst name actors in making a brief appearance in the project. He was joined on set by his *Vampire's Kiss* rival Judd Nelson as a cop, his 'brat pack' pals brothers Charlie Sheen (as a thief) and Emilio Estevez with Cary Elwes (as tow truck drivers). The 1988 film enjoyed the briefest of video releases before sinking without trace – although it's still an object of curiosity for fans of some of the actors involved.

The second oddball outing for Nic was playing the lead in an Italian war film entitled *Tempo di uccidere*, which was retitled for American audiences as *Time To Kill* or *The Short Cut* and briefly released on video to indifferent business in 1990. The Italian-made thriller featured Nic alongside Ricky Tognazzi and an Italian supporting cast under the direction of Giuliano Montaldo. It hardly ever appears on Nic's official filmography and the actor refuses to discuss it.

Both these outings were Nic's equivalent of giving Hollywood the finger. He'd been expected by agents. lawyers, critics and even audiences to follow up his crowd-pleasing turn in *Moonstruck* with further mainstream, if slightly edgy, performances. He refused to please anyone but himself. However individual Cage wanted to be, though, reality was about to catch up with him.

What he had to take into account now were the costs of maintaining his position, the upkeep of the building and the lifestyle that he had acquired with the proceeds of his first big financial success. Then Christina Fulton had a shock in store for the wild man of the movies – he was to be a father. The news of the pregnancy was a surprise for Nic, as like Patricia Arquette's it had been unplanned, and now he had to face whether to have a family. He and Christina decided to have the baby so now Nic had an imminent family to support as well as a large house. More and faster work in mainstream movies was the only answer. 'I had bought the house and got in over my head. I kept saying I should do a little movie that would be good for my soul, but I needed the money. I admit it. I was not being true to my instincts, but I felt like I wanted to do a role with a straight, American character.'

The result was *Fire Birds* or *Wings Of The Apache* as it was retitled in the United Kingdom. By the time of the casting in 1990 Nick was being represented by powerful agent Ed Limato, who was pushing him more and more towards mainstream fare, like

With Tommy Lee Jones in Fire Birds*, a macho action-adventure flop he starred in for financial reasons.*

this version of *Top Gun* with helicopters. Nic's co-stars in this macho action-adventure flick were to be Tommy Lee Jones and Sean Young. '*Fire Birds* was as unlikely for me as you could get,' Nic admitted. 'I was challenged by it and the people involved wanted to work with me. They made a deal that was respectable and made me feel good, got me out of some debts that I was severely into with the house.'

British director David Green was co-ordinating this tale of an American task force sent to a South American country to use their high-tech flying machines to battle drug barons. Laced in among the action sequences was a romance between Nicolas's character and Sean Young which never really seemed to catch fire – unlike many other things in the film.

Green had directed *Buster*, the story of one of the British 'great train robbers' from the sixties, starring Phil Collins, and *Fire Birds* was his first American movie. However, he knew just which actors his seemingly standard action fare needed: 'Nic was the leading man we wanted. He had youth appeal, as well as the look of an action man. He fitted his pilot's flying outfit. I think it was a new sort of show for him and he went for it, like a total professional. What I wanted from him was a very straightforward American hero-type guy, who goes out to beat the drug lords and overcomes his own problems and prejudices along the way. Cage did this extremely well.'

Whatever the merits or otherwise of *Fire Birds*, Green is to be credited with being first to spot Nic's potential as a film action hero. He seemed an unlikely candidate, but the film set up an image that Nic was not to fully exploit until some years later in his action movie trilogy of *The Rock, Con Air* and *Face/Off.*

However, while working on location in Tuscon, Arizona, Nic had more immediate concerns on his mind than his possible future as an action icon. He was in close contact with Christina, monitoring her pregnancy and weighing up in his own mind what to do next in his private life. He could marry Christina, but neither of them was keen, and he'd seen Patricia Arquette cope with a kid and a movie career without marrying. He sought advice from his co-stars, his director, the stunt co-ordinator, in fact anyone on the movie who'd give him the time of day. 'I'm about to be a dad,' Nic would tell people, 'I fear my life as a debauched playboy is over!'

Preoccupied Nic may have been, but director David Green set out not to let it get in the way of his performance or of the safety concerns on the film. Any movie featuring flying sequences – especially with helicopters – is a danger zone. Nic was gung-ho about what was required of him, but Green was on hand to make sure that all the safety concerns were met. 'There is a kid inside me who likes helicopters and fireworks,' Nic said gleefully, who thought the Apache attack helicopters were 'cool, because they look like some sort of winged predator, a wasp or something'.

Before arriving on location Nic, Young and Jones had all put in time on the army's own Apache flight simulator – an experience which simply reminded Nic of playing a computer game. 'The simulator is almost as difficult to fly as the actual Apache,' he claimed of his abortive attempts. 'I don't know if I even got it to hover off the ground. I kept crashing and tilting the machine, like in an arcade game.'

'We had more 'copters in the air than any film before,' Green claimed of the location stunt work required for the film. 'The number of helicopters that have crashed on movie sets is legendary.' But *Fire Birds* passed off without incident, and Nicolas and Tommy Lee Jones survived their efforts at doing their own stunts.

Nic's casting was one of the aspects of the film that annoyed the US Army adviser who worked on it. Along with the fact that a woman helicopter pilot like Sean Young was unlikely, Nic's slicked back hairstyle and laconic attitude were causing friction with the military. 'That really kinda rips me off a little bit,' said one of the Army colonels posted to the set. 'That's not realistic. He should look like a soldier!'

Nicolas was up front about the fact that he was setting out to be a different kind of action hero in *Fire Birds*. 'This straightforward American hero was a challenge,' he claimed, before admitting that he just couldn't resist tinkering with the character as it was conceived in the script. He set out to make Chief Warrant Officer Jake Preston 'kind of arrogant and a little vain, with insecurities'. In fact, he wanted to make his character a bit more like Nicolas Cage. 'It was the kind of thing I hadn't done before. It was something new for me. That turned me on, trying to play a straight American hero, which is the most challenging thing I could do. That was more of a chance than anything else, in my opinion, and I tried it on for size.'

Whether it was worry about the part he was playing, concerns about Christina's pregnancy and the change that was coming to his life, or just plain grumpiness, Nic was not fun to be around on the location shoot. 'He needs to be in this rage all day,'

For Firebirds *co-star Sean Young, Nic was reminiscent of Hollywood action star Harrison Ford.*

Sean Young said of her co-star and love interest. 'Not an "Aaaah!" rage, just an inner rage. But the thing about Nic is that he's not a chronic talker, in the sense that he doesn't need to take that rage out on you, he doesn't walk all over you.'

Young admitted to seeing him in terms of another all-round American movie icon. 'He reminds me a little of Harrison Ford. He doesn't need anyone outside the work, outside the action, the cut. A lot of actors need one another when they are both working. They need to spend time together, they need to work it out, they need to see what the other person is feeling, they need to be with that person in the bar, they just need . . .'

Needy or not, Nic finally decided he was out of place on *Fire Birds*. 'They were trying to do a rehash of *Top Gun* and I couldn't fit that bill,' he said, admitting defeat. 'I knew when the producers came into the trailer and said: "We want you to smile more" that I was miscast.' Although Nic boasts an expressive face, he does have a natural tendency to look mournful, even when he's happy. He was fed up with people – including co-star Sean Young – telling him to cheer up or lighten up.

Nic considered he'd grown up somewhat by the time he was making *Fire Birds*. He was now 26 and was beginning to leave some of the method-acting madness behind him. Taking the part home with him was not to be a symptom of the making of this movie. 'That's a problem young actors have,' Nic claimed. 'I'm too old for that. That way lies . . . madness. For the rest of my life I'll be the man who ate the cockroach. When I started acting all I knew about was people like Robert DeNiro gaining 50 pounds for a role, so I wanted to do that too. I learned after ten years of doing it that I don't need to do it . . . Some of the ridiculous things I did will always stay with me. I pulled my teeth out for *Birdy*, I jumped on a car for *Raising Arizona*, I ate a cockroach for *Vampire's Kiss* – but now I've grown up.'

Critical reaction and box office takings on both sides of the Atlantic were disappointing. Considering he thought the movie was poor, Hal Hinson, writing in the *Washington Post*, was somewhat taken by Nicolas Cage's performance. He called *Fire Birds* 'more video game than motion picture. There seems to be some sort of contest between Cage, who plays a maverick fighter ace, and Tommy Lee Jones, his flight instructor, for top billing in the category of skyrocketing weirdness. Ultimately Cage wins the battle by virtue of sheer florid excess. With his sleepy eyelids and Modigliani face, this bonkers star looks more like a cartoon wolf than a conventional leading man. And at times he seems to nearly twirl his lines around his head as if he were doing rope tricks with them. Cage is a magnetic presence.'

In Britain, where the change of title to *Wings Of The Apache* was in the hope that no-one would connect it with the US flop, the film fared little better. *Empire* magazine said: 'Cage looks terminally bored in a finale which busily packs in a lot of action without ever e/ven getting close to exciting.' The film took around $14.8 million at the United States box office, far behind the $80 million taken by *Moonstruck* or even the $23 million gross for *Raising Arizona*. It was a poor return on the $22 million investment in the movie. Nic's first attempt at a mainstream action flick had been a dismal flop. 'I enjoyed it,' protested the star. 'It is what it is, a very pro-action adventure film, which is fine, it has its place.'

If ever there were an 'alternative Hollywood' match made in heaven it was that between Nicolas Cage and writer-director David Lynch. Since taking five years to complete his film school project *Eraserhead*, David Lynch has ploughed his own idiosyncratic furrow through Hollywood, turning out such *grand guignol* creepy confections as *The Elephant Man*, with John Hurt and Anthony Hopkins; the flawed film version of Frank Herbert's sci-fi epic *Dune*; suburban oddity *Blue Velvet* with Dennis Hopper and Kyle MacLachlan; and the briefly popular but ultimately overextended TV series and film spin-off, *Twin Peaks*.

In 1990 Lynch was planning to make what he initially called a 'little character study' called *Wild At Heart*. Based on a book by Barry Gifford, the $10 million film was quickly put into development when Lynch took a liking to the source novel while he was struggling with an entirely different project for Britain's Propaganda Films. The film is a dark and delirious road movie, following the adventures of ex-con Sailor Ripley and twenty-year-old sexpot Lula Fortune as they travel across America on an odyssey that contains strong echoes of *The Wizard Of Oz*. The wicked witch on their trail is Diane Ladd (Laura Dern's real-life mother) and her entourage of hired hitmen, out to get Sailor.

Nic came up with a unique interpretation of the character of Sailor Ripley, and discovered that it fitted right in with David Lynch's own off-kilter vision of the film. For once Nic's bizarre take on a character worked out perfectly. He decided to play Sailor not as a real person, but as a cartoon character, a 2-D version of Elvis Presley. He even

Nic Cage and Laura Dern brought Sailor and Lulu to irrepressible life in David Lynch's Wild At Heart.

wore his own personal snakeskin jacket throughout the film. 'Deciding to play him as Elvis was a weird thing to do,' he admitted, 'because at that time it was taboo to use imitation. In the book *An Actor Prepares* [the method-acting handbook] by Stanislavski, it says that the worst thing an actor can do is to copy another performer. I had always believed that, but then with *Wild At Heart*, I thought, maybe it's time to try something else. I used to call that my Andy Warhol period, because I would take the icon of Elvis the way Warhol would and try to put something on top of it and filter it in some way.'

Despite the extremes of his portrayal, Nic believed he was sticking to his desire to avoid too much method acting and to tone down the weirdness of his character. 'I've often played roles that were very large and sort of manic,' he said, 'and I wondered how I could be that ludicrous, but in a very contained way. Sailor is a lot more sedate than I've been in a film for a while. He's a strong character who doesn't need to rant and rave to get attention. The challenge is to be megacool in a way that will be totally absurd.' In fact, in *Wild At Heart*, Nic's character is almost the most normal one in a weird and wonderful bunch made up of typical David Lynch oddballs, played by a quirky cast which includes Willem Dafoe, Isabella Rossellini,

Harry Dean Stanton, Cage's pal Crispin Glover and musician John Lurie.

'Nic's got nerve,' noted David Lynch of his star performer. 'It's amazing how much courage it takes to say certain things, and he's got that courage. At one point while we were shooting I told Nic he was going to sing opera. The idea was that he awoke in the night from having this dream about a cotton ball, and then sure enough there was one under his bed, and he leans down to it and starts singing opera to a single, lone, moonlit cotton ball in the darkness. Now, there are not a lot of people you could talk to about that who would really grab hold of it, but Nic just lit up like a Christmas tree.'

Nic was inspired by the character of Sailor in a way he hadn't been since playing Peter Loew in *Vampire's Kiss*. 'All I kept thinking was he's not red wine, he's motor oil. He's an old Corvette that needs a tune up, wearing a snakeskin jacket,' was his typically out-there view of his character. 'He can break down but when you drive him, it feels good. Those ideas kept me in character.' He got on extremely well with his young co-star Laura Dern, which is just as well as their sexual encounters punctuate the film repeatedly. In fact, some people thought the pair were getting on a little too well. Nic denied anything but a professional involvement with Dern, who was going out with actor Jeff Goldblum at the time. 'For the record, we're good friends,' Nic claimed. 'Lovers we're not. We're dealing with a movie here that is extremely sexual and you can imagine the stories that generates.'

A requirement of the part was for Nic to sing, something he'd never tackled before. He laid down a spaced-out version of *Love Me Tender*, which he then mimed

Nic Cage and Willem Dafoe lit up the screen in the decidedly off-kilter Wild At Heart.

to on the soundstage for one scene in the movie. During shooting, despite the fakery of the performance, the atmosphere got the better of the many extras crowding out the club scene, who wildly applauded Cage and mobbed the actor for autographs, before an assistant director intervened to clear them away. It was a moment which brought a smile to David Lynch's face.

A visit to the Cannes film festival in the South of France in May 1990 also brought a smile to the director's face. Lynch finished post-production on *Wild At Heart* just weeks before the festival where he hoped to premiere the film. He reportedly received a final print of the movie the day before he and Isabella Rossellini were due to depart. In fact, the cans of film were taken on the plane as hand luggage. 'We were right up to the wire,' revealed Lynch. 'The gentleman at Swiss Air was very upset, but finally he let it happen, because it did fit under the seat.' It was worth all the effort as the movie played to an ecstatic audience and scooped the prestigious Palme D'Or, top prize at the festival. 'I was very surprised that it won,' claimed Lynch. 'Thrilled, but surprised.' The award upset some of the strong local French contingent who had expected the Gerard Depardieu vehicle *Cyrano De Bergerac* to walk away with the prize, which, before *Wild At Heart*, had rarely been awarded to American movies.

But despite winning the prize, *Wild At Heart* was subject to wildly varying reviews when it was released on both sides of the Atlantic in August 1990. Some people complained of the film being too violent, despite the fact that some scenes had been removed and some reshot by Lynch to remove some gratuitous nastiness. Others complained of the upfront sexuality of the film, although again, Lynch had had to reign himself in while making the movie to curb the excesses of Laura Dern and Nicolas Cage.

Roger Ebert, film critic of the *Chicago Sun-Times*, wrote: 'The movie is lurid melodrama, soap opera, exploitation, put-on and self-satire. Cage, whose character is the local version of Elvis Presley crossed with James Dean and Tab Hunter, looks like a villain in a silent movie and does a conscious imitation of Presley in all of his dialogue, and even bursts into song a couple of times.' Hal Hinson, in the *Washington Post*, also commented on Nic's take on Elvis: 'Cage enters into a wild parody of the limp-shouldered early Elvis, speaking his lines with a mumbled-low, "'scuse me, ma'am" accent. He wedges the King's later Vegas moves in there too, thrusting and kick-boxing against invisible opponents. This is amyl nitrite acting – the Method on poppers.'

And the infamous snakeskin jacket that Cage brought to the character of Sailor Ripley – what happened to that after the film? 'I gave it to Laura [Dern]. But for my birthday my father bought me a jacket made out of cork, a cork jacket. It's like leather, really strange . . .'

Not long after the Cannes prize Nic was responsible for a stupid incident on board a commuter flight from Los Angeles to San Francisco. He was on board US Air flight 407, preparing to land at San Francisco airport on 20 July 1990 and he'd had too much to drink.

Bored, Cage made use of the public address system next to the stewardesses' station to announce to the entire plane that he was the captain, he was feeling unwell and was about to lose control of the plane. What possessed him to launch such a daft prank is not clear. 'I was bored and I wanted to liven up the flight,' he offered weakly as an excuse. 'I had a few drinks and wanted a bit of fun. I meant it as a joke, but everyone started freaking out and screaming.'

Nic's bizarre behaviour alienated the passengers and crew, many of whom were shocked to see a well-known Hollywood actor acting the goat on a commercial flight. 'It was a bad experience,' deadpanned Nic, who faced arrest when the plane descended into San Francisco. 'I got carried away – I didn't think the PA system was connected to the entire plane. The crew told me I could be arrested when I got off the plane, and sure enough there were three policemen waiting for me.'

Nic faced charges of creating a disturbance, but the airline declined to press criminal charges, although the way was still open for the Federal Aviation Authority to bring civil charges against him. He had to turn on the charm to talk his way out of the situation. 'I explained that I was just having a bit of fun and told them I was very, very sorry. After a lot of talking they let me off with a very stern warning – I was very lucky not to end up in jail.'

The seriousness of the possible charges Nic faced were summed up by San Francisco airport police sergeant James O'Donnell. 'If someone had been injured in the panic, then it could have been a different story and Cage would definitely have been prosecuted. You can go away for a long time for something like that.'

His potential for criminal behaviour had in fact been lurking at the back of Nic's mind since his teenage years. Despite his comfortable middle-class and intellectual family background, he had always felt like something of a tearaway, growing up in a family where rock music had been regarded as something of a 'sin'. The teenage Nicolas might have been drawn to a life of crime, had it not been for acting. 'It's been my ticket to freedom,' claimed the actor. 'I can't ever bad-mouth acting. It gave me a way out, both psychologically and financially. I think if it wasn't for acting, I would probably be dead. It's been a tremendous outlet for anger and bad feelings. I would probably have turned to crime.'

Nic had been feeling stressed out in both his professional and personal lives, and it was this stress which had contributed to the incident on the airplane. *Fire Birds* had flopped dismally, but *Wild At Heart* was promising to be a huge critical success, if not a particularly big commercial hit. Nic found the public perception of him quite baffling – from being criticised as a bad actor in *Vampire's Kiss* to being hailed as a cultural icon in *Wild At Heart*, he found it hard to relate the perceptions people had of him to his real, inner life. Christina was pregnant and expecting his child at the end of 1990 – and he'd finally decided not to marry her. They both had too much going on in their careers, although they both decided to take responsibility for the upbringing of the child.

Variety was the spice of Nic's life. 'I want to be the kind of actor who does a little bit of everything,' he said of his ever-varied career. 'Elia Kazan [director of one of Cage's favourite movies, *East Of Eden*] told me once just to mix it up, keep doing new things. It's more exciting. It may not be bankable. It may not be the way for an audience to get to know an actor or to imitate them, like Stallone or Eastwood. But I get turned on just creating somebody new and living with that person for a while.'

Somebody new and important came into Cage's life on 26 December 1990. 'He's my sunshine,' Nic said of his son, who was named Weston Coppola Cage. He and Christina were delighted, and although Nic had tried to mentally prepare himself for becoming a father, the reality of the situation was overwhelming. He talked a lot to Patricia Arquette about the birth of her son Enzo, finding out what having a child had meant to her. Changes in his lifestyle were inevitable, but Cage was determined to balance being an actor with being a father. He found himself calming down a lot, almost in spite of himself. His hell-raising days with Sean Penn and Jim Carrey were pretty much over, making his bizarre behaviour on the Los Angeles to San Francisco flight his last fling.

'It brings a new kind of emotion, a new depth that wasn't there before,' he said of fatherhood and its effect on him. 'I'm always aware that what I do could affect my son. You don't want to wake up hung over when you have a child. Being a father has had more of an impact on my life than anything else before or since. One of the amazing things about children is that they automatically cut out any of the debauchery or decadence left over from your youth. As soon as Weston was born, I stopped smoking cigarettes and started buckling my seat-belt. My lifestyle became dramatically different, just by nature of becoming a parent.'

Nic's childhood friend Jeff Levine saw the change in the actor from the time his son was born. 'He's become the sedate, responsible father guy. When we get together now, we watch movies and talk about spouses and children. Just boring, grown up stuff.' Levine had worked as Nic's personal assistant on many of his movies and appeared alongside his long-time friend in many of them, often in blink-and-you'll-miss-him bit parts.

This new maturity was something Nic himself was keen to talk about, seeing an opportunity to put some of the method acting excesses he'd indulged in firmly behind him. 'I've grown up,' he admitted. 'When I was young I was pretty rebellious, but now in my life I'm pretty normal. I save the wild stuff for movies. What I'm into is pretty boring.'

He developed a new career strategy, determined to leave some of the weirdness he'd indulged himself in firmly in the past. 'Everyone thought I was crazy,' he said of his earlier roles. 'I mean, even smart people in Hollywood, people who cast movies. They thought I wore snakeskin jackets, or I had a wooden hand or that I did eat bugs!' Nic was hoping to be cast in a comedy, but other things cropped up first.

6. Jimmy Stewart from Mars

AFTER *WILD AT HEART*, NIC reteamed with Laura Dern to play Sailor and Lulu once again in a 50-minute TV special directed by Lynch called *Industrial Symphony No. 1: The Dream Of The Broken Hearted*. Cage played the 'Heartbreaking Man'. He also went on to narrate a 1992 episode of *American Heroes And Legends* on the subject of Davy Crockett. TV was providing filler roles and occasional work – like the voice-over – but Nic was determined to return to features. He was keen to explore on film what he was experiencing in his own life: 'My son changed my whole life. Babies are a tremendous life-changing force. They bring good luck. Weston's taught me there is such a thing as happiness. Being a dad has exposed me to a whole new range of emotions. I'd like to explore them on film.' Moreover, Nic was worried about his decision not to marry Christina and the ramifications, which led them to split up. He was keen to ensure that Weston grew up with a mother around, so he and Christina worked out a complicated custody arrangement which neither party is keen to discuss. The practical side of the agreement meant that both parents got to spend plenty of time with Weston, both alone and together.

His sexual relationship with Christina now over, Nic was a free agent again. Although he didn't indulge himself as much as when he broke off with Jenny Wright, he was keen to get out and meet people again. After all, he was more famous now after *Wild At Heart* than ever before – and the passionate nature of the role of Sailor Ripley was bound to attract attention to him. 'Sex is my religion,' he had once claimed. 'It's a miracle. One of the few miracles of life. I want sex to feel like I'm at the edge of a cliff and I can just fall down into her . . . that's happened maybe twice.'

It was this liberated frame of mind that lead Nic to *Zandalee*. Seeking a new relationship, he felt he could bring something of his real-life situation to the movie. 'Sometimes my choices have nothing to do with what would be a good movie. If I'm going through a bad period in my life, I might get that role to exorcise it. Take *Zandalee*. That was a movie I made which was a very dark example of sexuality – something that I was living through – and I wanted to express it. I wouldn't have done it if I had not been getting betrayed in my own personal life. I wanted to be the "other guy".'

In the would-be erotic melodrama Nic played an artist who starts an affair with the wife of his best friend. The wife was blonde British actress Erika Anderson, a one-time model and a DJ for the National Public Radio station in Tulsa, Oklahoma. The driving force behind the film was, surprisingly, actor Judge Reinhold. Not only did he take the role of Nic's best friend, Thierry, but he was also the producer of the film. *Zandalee* was a dramatic departure for Reinhold, who was better known as Eddie Murphy's slapstick sidekick in the *Beverly Hills Cop* movies. He saw *Zandalee* as an escape route from the comedy rut he'd been trapped in for years.

Thierry is a burned out Southern poet, who has inherited his father's business in New Orleans, but is wasting his talent, preferring instead to spend his time repressing his sexy wife Zandalee (Anderson). Nic's character – long haired, moustachioed and sporting a ridiculous goatee beard – was Johnny, a wild-at-heart painter.

The film followed in the footsteps of the late eighties genre of glossy erotica which emerged after the success of the Kim Basinger–Mickey Rourke hit *9½ Weeks* and Zalman King's *Wild Orchid*. This $7 million independent addition to the genre had one notable difference – it was written by a woman, Mari Kornhauser. She viewed the film as a kind of *Last Tango In New Orleans*, even going so far as to coin the phrase 'sex-*noir*' to sum it up.

Directing the sex-with-emotion scenes was New Zealander Sam Pillsbury, who saw the film as a chance to lampoon American uptightness. 'You'd be crazy to make a picture like this and not expect a really violent response to it,' he admitted on the New Orleans location shoot. 'I don't have a hell of a lot of worry if a large percentage of the population finds this a shocking movie. In a way, the movie is a "fuck you" to that kind of response anyway.'

The idea for the movie came to Kornhauser when she was suffering from writer's block. She started work on a movie script with a collaborator, but got bogged down in the middle and started writing *Zandalee* simply as an exercise to get her creative juices flowing again. 'I've always been interested in pornographic literature,' confessed Kornhauser, who like Pillsbury saw the project as a statement on censorship. 'It's about an area of American society that I wanted to explore, not only in terms of censorship. This story is a morality tale – it's not *Emmanuelle*.'

Nic saw *Zandalee* as a distraction from his real-life woes and a final fling in the method-acting darkness before he achieved his long-held ambition of making a comedy. His career route seemed to be taking him in the opposite direction of his co-star Judge Reinhold. It was the straightforwardness of the sexual content that drew him to *Zandalee*: 'There are the most sex scenes in a movie that I have ever seen. It's just chock-full of sex. I think the director doesn't want it to have, like, the lyrical edge to it that most sex scenes have. I think he wants it to look like reality. He almost shot it in a way that was documentary at times. Sex is a good memory. People don't take Polaroids . . . or maybe some do. But you know, real lovemaking exists, and instead of lacing it with saccharine bullshit, he would rather do the movie in a literal way, in a real way, where the sex is a celebration of the moment and not hidden under a lot of fancy lighting and everything.'

For Nicolas, *Zandalee* was more than just a porn movie. As well as tackling the sexual content in a straightforward manner, he believed the role he was playing gave him a chance to expand his range of characters, to try out something new. It was a challenge to bring another of his comic-book rogues to celluloid life. 'I think that Johnny is a sort of vampire of innocence. He wants to corrupt innocence, because it is very seductive to him. He wants to push all his impulses to the edge, like an orange-juice machine extracting the juice. He's almost like a messenger of temptation.'

However, whatever deeper virtues the makers saw in it, *Zandalee* was widely disparaged by reviewers and flopped at the box office. It did, though, pick up a cult following upon its video release. Britain's *Mail On Sunday* review was typical: 'Nicolas Cage goes into emotional apoplexy . . . at least his no-holds barred acting is entertaining – there's not much else to laugh at.'

As a final fling for the Nicolas Cage weirdness, *Zandalee* was perfectly offbeat. 'It was a different kind of role than I'd played before, and it's exciting for me to portray a character who is not out there, not evil, but, uh, amoral.'

Returning from the sexual gymnastics and overwrought emotions of *Zandalee*, Nicolas Cage found himself involved in a real-life tempestuous relationship, with young model Kristen Zang. Nic met the eighteen-year-old when he was nightclubbing and the pair spent many nights out together, before she finally moved in with him into his Hollywood Hills castle.

Nic was continuing his search for the perfect relationship – and unlike many other young Hollywood actors, he would enter relationships seriously and give them every chance to work. He'd spent several years with both Jenny Wright and Christina Fulton, and was maintaining a friendly relationship with Christina after their split. In his heart, he was still carrying the torch for Patricia Arquette, but he wasn't ready yet to admit it to himself. Instead, he threw himself into a new life, looking after Weston during the day and clubbing with Kristen when his son was with Christina.

Nic found, however, he wasn't as keen on the clubbing life as he'd once been. Instead of going at it full on, he found he'd rather talk than dance – and dance floor fights were certainly out of the question. During one night out Nic was challenged in a night club by one of Kristen's ex-boyfriends. Nic was with Julian Lennon when he was suddenly struck in the face. Looking up he saw Guy Oseary – later to become the youthful president of Maverick Records, the label Madonna records for. At first he thought Oseary was playing a practical joke, but then realised that Kristen's ex-boyfriend was challenging him to a fight. 'I started to get up,' said Nic, who automatically fell back on his reflexes, before thinking twice about it. 'He walked away,' he said of Oseary. 'He's a kid, basically. I felt bad for him actually. I know if I do fight, I fight to kill. My motto had always been: maximum violence immediately. That means pushing the nose into the face or whatever you've got to do. So, I don't want to get into a fight.'

Nic with girlfriend Kristen Zang at the Golden Globe awards, 1993.

By 1992, with a two-year-old son, Nic was clearly mellowing. However, he hadn't lost his suspicions of the women he was involved with – for good reason. Nic believed Jenny Wright and Christina Fulton had gone out with other people behind his back towards the end of their relationships. He reacted to their betrayals and used the emotional turmoil to good effect in his performances in two very different ways in two very different movies – *Moonstruck* and *Zandalee*. The fear that Kristen Zang would do the same to him was always at the forefront of his mind and contributed to the quick demise of what was to be a short-lived and rocky relationship.

It was a request from his grandmother Divi – Louise Vogelsang – that finally brought Nic to a series of offbeat comedies. She felt that her grandson had not made any films she felt she could really enjoy, and after the excesses of *Zandalee*, Nic was inclined to agree. Perhaps it was time to turn to something lighter, to make something populist like *Moonstruck* or *Raising Arizona*, but with a slightly less zany, more mainstream approach to his performance.

'I neglected doing comedies for some time,' he recalled of his return to playing it for laughs. 'Part of it was that I didn't want to acknowledge that side of myself. I knew it was there, though. Is it pretentious to be always brooding, always an upset and angry guy? I knew I could be funny, but I didn't want to be. I still wanted to be James Dean – but that was a turning point, when I decided to tap into comedy.'

So instead of being James Dean, Nicolas Cage found the chance to become something more like James Stewart. His *Wild At Heart* director David Lynch had been dubbed 'Jimmy Stewart from Mars' by *The Elephant Man*'s producer, Mel Brooks, for having normal looks, but with a constant undercurrent of weirdness. It was a description that could just as easily, and perhaps more appropriately, be attached to Nicolas Cage, especially after what he called his 'sunshine trilogy' of *Honeymoon In Vegas, Guarding Tess* and *It Could Happen To You.*

Nic went all out to change his image, to win lighter roles and make himself more appealing to the Hollywood film industry movers and shakers, but he knew from the start it was not going to be easy. 'My agent even said *Honeymoon In Vegas* was a long shot,' he remembered, as he considered going up for the leading role. 'Rick Moranis would have fitted better. It was a bit of a sell, because there wasn't a whole lot in my work that would suggest I could play this everyday, ordinary guy. I had to kind of lobby for it.'

The 'everyday, ordinary guy' was private detective Jack Singer who, under duress, promises his dying mother (Anne Bancroft) he will not marry. It's a promise which doesn't reassure his girlfriend Betsy (Sarah Jessica Parker) who is keen to tie the knot. She gives Singer an ultimatum – get married or get lost. Once more under duress, Singer sets off with Betsy to Las Vegas for a quick wedding, only to lose her in a poker game to mob boss James Caan. Writer-director Andrew Bergman's madcap comedy charts Singer's increasingly fraught attempts to win Betsy back.

He may not have seemed like ideal casting to Bergman at first, but in the finished film it's hard to imagine anyone but Nicolas Cage bringing the right level of off-kilter ordinariness and weird intensity to the role. Both James Caan and Sarah Jessica Parker were attached to the film early on, while Bergman began a search for the right leading man. 'There were a few people I thought of, Billy Crystal – maybe a little bit too old. Then I heard Nic had read it. I'd never met him; my image of him was from these movies, that he'd be this very "out there" kind of guy.'

Bergman wanted to be convinced that Nic could handle the role and asked the actor to try out for the film in a screen test. He hadn't done that since *Moonstruck*, when MGM and Norman Jewison wanted to be sure he wasn't going to steal their film from Cher. 'Nic wasn't exactly what I had pictured for it, but he had a passion about him,' said Bergman of the casting. 'He came in, he read and he *was* this guy. I was surprised when he first presented himself for the role because it was odd. He had done such odd things, but he read and he was sensational.'

Suddenly, being normal seemed very attractive to Cage. 'My character in this movie still finds himself in a wild, manic situation after everything starts to go haywire on him, so it's not like I'm selling out or anything,' claimed the wanna-be mainstream actor. 'I've had a sort of passing, if you will, of playing offbeat characters. I don't know if it's because the characters are offbeat or once I get my hands on them they become offbeat, but Jack Singer is a normal guy, whatever "normal" is, who just happens to find himself in a ridiculous situation.'

It should have come as a surprise to no one that Andrew Bergman and Nicolas Cage would hit it off. Bergman had enjoyed his biggest hit as a writer with the Mel Brooks comedy *Blazing Saddles*, twenty years before *Honeymoon In Vegas*. He'd avoided mainstream hits, though all his films had made money, turning down the chance to direct *My Cousin Vinny* and *City Slickers*. 'I have a great nose for turning down blockbusters,' admitted Bergman, placing himself in the same category as his leading man.

Bergman wrote the script to meet 'a desire to do a boy-girl story and a desire to do something with a less arcane plot than usual. On top of that, all this other stuff got layered in: who Jack meets, what happens to him – all pretty much along the lines of ordinary people, or as ordinary as Nic Cage can be, falling into hideous circumstances.'

The 'hideous circumstances' begin when the high-stakes gambler Tommy Korman (James Caan) sees Betsy in Vegas and because she is the spitting image of his late wife, the high stakes gambler just has to have her. Luring dopey Jack Singer into a card game, and then into a $60,000-deep hole, he makes an 'indecent proposal' to him. This is to write off the debt for a weekend with Betsy. Singer agrees reluctantly, but changes his mind when he realises the couple are off to Hawaii and Korman plans a more permanent relationship with her. 'It's like they're shooting two different movies,' Nic said on the film's Las Vegas location. 'One where there's snorkelling and horses and sunsets, and the other where I'm getting the bum steers and being put in jail.' Nic excels in the role of the not-so-smart ordinary guy caught up in an extraordinary situation. It was the flipside of his more usual parts – the extraordinary guy who struggles with ordinary, everyday life.

The film was made on a tough schedule. Shooting began in August 1991 with one week's location filming in New York City and two weeks' interiors on a sound stage in Los Angeles' Culver Studios. The cast and crew then spent four weeks on location in Las Vegas, and although it was difficult for Nic to be separated from Weston, he actually enjoyed his time away from Christina and even from Kristen. The change of scenery gave him a fresh outlook and the chance to recover from the break-up with Fulton and the dark depths of *Zandalee*. It all helped feed into an upbeat, angst-free performance.

In Las Vegas Nic plunged into the potential addiction of gambling and played the gaming tables for big stakes. Day by day his bets climbed, reaching the giddy heights of $10,000 on one. This excessiveness was upsetting his co-star Sarah Jessica Parker, but Nic claimed he couldn't help himself. After losing the cash, he spent an hour running on the treadmill in his hotel room in an effort to feel better. The following morning he sneaked down to the tables once again, won back his money and stopped gambling. The experience had served as something of a wake-up call, showing him just how easy it would be to slip into habits that could have cost him dear.

Honeymoon In Vegas climaxes with a horde of skydiving Elvises being joined by Jack Singer. This was becoming something of a trademark – it was the third time that

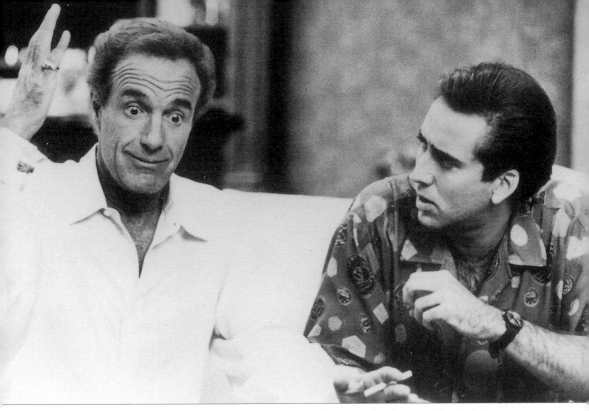

Mob boss Tommy Korman makes an 'indecent proposal' to Nic's hapless gambler, Jack Singer, in Honeymoon In Vegas.

Nic found himself impersonating Elvis. 'For a while the Elvis thing was just happening,' he said of the triple bill of *Wild At Heart*, an appearance as Elvis on TV in *Saturday Night Live* and now in *Honeymoon In Vegas*. 'It was a little scary because they never dropped the accent,' he said of being surrounded by fifteen to twenty people all of whom thought they were Elvis. 'I think they saw me as one of their own. I'm not sure whether I like that or not – I can't see myself being another person for my entire life. There was a guy there, a very sweet guy named Dave Elvis. We had a nice cigar when he finished working and I like him, but he never dropped the accent.'

In fact, as shooting wore on, and despite his own liking for Elvis – Nic saw the singer's rise and fall as something of an American myth – he decided he really didn't want to hang out with the multiple Elvises any more than he had to. They'd talk to him about his playing Elvis: '"Helll-ooo, Nicky, you did a heck of an Elvis in *Wild At Heart*. When you finish here today, whaddya say we talk a little about E? You know, we'll just shoot the shit about E." I'm really gonna wrap here and go and have a beer and talk about Elvis with these guys? I mean, it would have been interesting, but wrong movie,' said Nic.

Honeymoon In Vegas won Nic a Golden Globe nomination as Best Actor in a Comedy or Musical. However, despite the new mainstream success he was enjoying, some critics were still inclined to claim that he couldn't really act and was only

91

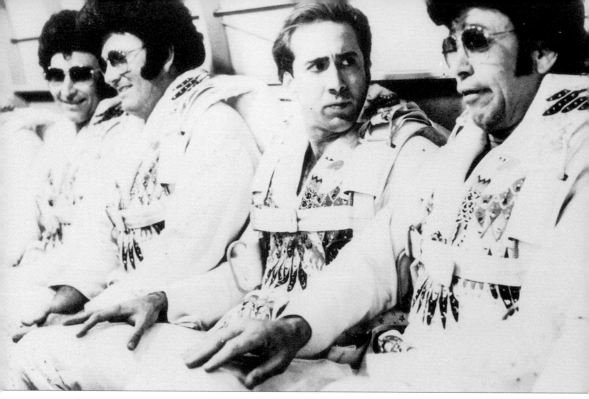

Playing Elvis yet again, Nic finds himself about to skydive into Las Vegas in a last-ditch attempt to prevent his girlfriend from marrying a mobster.

making it in the business because he was a Coppola. 'I don't think anybody at this point thinks I can't act,' he countered. '*Honeymoon In Vegas* did not make $50 million because Francis is my uncle,' he laughed, finally putting the Coppola connection which had hung over his career behind him.

Having sorted our his finances after the purchase of the gothic castle in Hollywood, Nic was in a spending mood once again. Cars now replaced motorbikes as an obsession. In the garage of the castle sat a silver Peugeot convertible which had once been owned by 'rat pack' member Dean Martin. Also in Nic's car collection were a black Porsche, a 1967 blue Corvette Stingray Coupe, a Lamborghini, a Ferrari and a 1967 Chevelle.

Nic didn't need all those cars, but the ability to buy them meant much more to him. 'I admit I like having the ability to buy these cars. The money also allows me to make low budget movies for no pay.' His money had also gone into expensive additions for the house, including Murano glass on the coffee table in his living room and more art for his walls.

Cage's next couple of films were to be in that 'low budget movies for no pay' category. *Honeymoon In Vegas* director Andrew Bergman had promised him the pair would work again, telling him 'I have something at Fox, a little cop picture'. It would be a while before they'd be able to make it, so Nic filled in with a few minor roles.

Both the dectective thriller *Deadful* and the comedy-drama *Amos and Andrew* were forgettable little movies which did nothing to further Nic's career but were hardly seen by enough people to damage it. Nic was unhappy at having been passed over for a role in *The Godfather, Part 3*, so the Coppola family were not top of his Christmas card list. However, the chance to work with his film director brother Christopher Coppola on *Deadfall* was too much to ignore. Cage played a disguise-obsessed hitman who is heavily into fifties culture. 'It was a chance to work with Christopher,' he said of the movie which flopped at the box office and didn't even make any impact on video. 'He let me go for it, in the regard that I could have fun with make-up and disguise myself so I could really take advantage of the opportunity.' It was a flashback to the brothers' amateur movie-making during their childhood.

Christopher Coppola had managed to assemble a decent cast for *Deadfall*, the story of two men caught in a dangerous con game. Co-starring with Nic were James Cameron favourite Michael Biehn, veteran James Coburn, brat pack regular Charlie Sheen, sixties burnout Peter Fonda and Nic's aunt, Talia Shire.

Amos And Andrew also looked like a good idea on paper, but the film proved to be something else entirely. Director E. Max Frye (writer of Jonathan Demme's *Something Wild*) intended the film to be a social satire concerning the average American's perceptions about race, but the finished work is misjudged and misguided. Samuel L. Jackson – later to make a bigger impact in *Pulp Fiction, Die Hard With A Vengeance* and *The Long Kiss Goodnight* – played professional playwright Andrew Sterling, a black man who moves into a exclusive white island neighbourhood, only to be taken by local neighbours for a burglar. When the police, led by Dabney Coleman, playing an incompetent chief up for election as Commissioner, and trigger-happy dope Brad Dourif attack Sterling in his home and the mistake is realised, the Chief plans an audacious plot to get him out of the mess. Nic played Amos Odell, a small time thief and misfit who had been arrested earlier and is sent in by the Chief to pretend to take Sterling hostage. When Nic realises he's been set up by the police to take the fall for their mistakes, he sets out to help Jackson get his revenge.

From the opening mistaken-identity robbery through to the hostage crisis, *Amos And Andrew* plays tragedy for farce, but is never extreme enough to be truly funny. The heavy handed satire strikes out at pot-smoking liberals, dumb cops, the news media and reality-based TV shows with a scatter-gun approach that hits few of the targets effectively. Although slickly made, with Jackson good as the paranoid playwright and Nic livening things up considerably even though he gives a somewhat subdued performance, *Amos And Andrew* is an example of how what seems like a smart idea can end up being a less than inspiring film. The *Village Voice* noted of the film: 'Cage is likeable in spite of his limited role.'

Adjusting to his new domestic arrangements had been tough enough, but to have his career drift off course was worrying for the actor. He was just a year away from beginning work on his Oscar-winning role in *Leaving Las Vegas*, but he had more comedy to tackle first in *It Could Happen to You* and *Guarding Tess*.

7. Out of the Sun

NICOLAS CAGE WAS NOW DISCOVERING that comedy was his forte. Despite misgivings over the hit-and-miss nature of the genre, especially after *Amos And Andrew*, he was keen to continue in this vein in the hope of recreating the unparalleled mainstream success of *Honeymoon In Vegas*.

The next success, however, came along in very different shape, as the *film noir* thriller *Red Rock West*. It didn't look like it at the time of release, however, as the finished film was dumped on TV cable network Home Box Office (HBO) and released on video before finally enjoying a belated theatrical release in 1994. It then received great notices. *New York* magazine's critic David Denby called the film 'The best American movie released so far in 1994.' But when the $6 million thriller was being made in late 1992 and early 1993, Nic didn't have high hopes. He saw it as being the third in what looked to be a trilogy of poor choices.

Director John Dahl had mapped out a genre he dubbed 'cowboy *noir*' with his 1989 film *Kill Me Again*, which starred Joanne Whalley-Kilmer, Val Kilmer and Michael Madsen. The film enjoyed a limited release and was a moderate success – enough to win him backing for a second feature. It was while scouting locations in rural Nevada for that movie that Dahl developed the ideas which were to become *Red Rock West*. 'I came upon a number of towns that had definitely seen better days,' he said. 'That was when the idea first came to me, of what would happen if a guy walked into some little bar in some little town and was mistaken for someone else?'

Co-written with his brother Rick, Dahl's *Red Rock West* is a strong vehicle for Nic, casting him as an out-of-work drifter who gets in over his head when he stops off in a small Wyoming town. A heated mixture of greed, betrayal, mistaken identity and revenge, *Red Rock West* proved Dahl to be a strong director of strong actors, getting a toned-down performance from Nic as the resourceful fall guy, and putting such colourful actors as Dennis Hopper and J. T. Walsh in strong supporting roles. He even drew a dramatically edgy performance from *Twin Peaks* starlet Lara Flynn Boyle, to the surprise of many.

Cage was very taken with his character, Michael, someone whose moral ambiguities he could relate to. 'Michael's a very ambiguous character, a survivalist. He's not a great thinker, but he has a lot of integrity. He's one of those guys that's about an inch away from becoming a thief, but he's conflicted by his moral code. A lot of things happen on account of money and what people will do to get it. The

95

greed is Michael's conflict. He's the moral force in a very dark situation.'

Set over a period of two days, *Red Rock West* took a total of seven weeks to make. Shooting began in December 1992 in Wilcox, Arizona, an hour outside of Tuscon. The town, with the railroad running parallel to the Main Street, was ideal for the needs of the production, although a lot of work was required on abandoned buildings to make the Red Rock Sheriff's office and the local bar, where much of the action takes place.

After three weeks in Arizona, the cast and crew returned to Los Angeles for the remaining four weeks of production. A warehouse across the street from the County Jail in downtown Los Angeles served as a soundstage for the interiors of Wayne and Suzanne's house. The most elaborate set constructed, though, was a cemetery featured at the climax of the movie. Within a hangar at Santa Monica Airport, the art department built a full-scale burial ground, using 20,000 cubic feet of earth. A week was spent here, filming the movie's graphic final fight scenes, with both Nic and co-star Dennis Hopper performing their own stunts.

However, *Red Rock West* was not deemed to be suitable for movie theatres, according to Columbia Tristar, the studio who'd financed it. To the great disappointment of the director and star alike, the taut little melodrama studded with unforgettable characters and full of plot twists was dubbed by a studio executive as 'unreleaseable'.

Columbia Tristar inexplicably wrote off their $6 million investment in the picture and sold it on to HBO, who ran the television broadcast and arranged an American video release. They also released it for cinemas in foreign territories, and it was only when the film made a significant impact abroad that it crept back to North America. After doing good business in France, it was screened at the Toronto International Film Festival and then picked up by the programmer for San Francisco's Haight-Ashbury art house cinema, the Roxie. After breaking house records, *Red Rock West* played limited but lucrative engagements around the country during 1994.

By the time *Red Rock West* became a critical and commercial hit, Nic had moved back to comedy. The second film in his 'sunshine trilogy' was *Guarding Tess*, in which he played bodyguard Doug Chesnic, entrusted with looking after a particularly irascible First Lady, played with great aplomb by veteran actress Shirley McLaine.

Finishing a three-year tour of duty, Chesnic is looking for some action, but he finds himself transferred back to his task protecting the ex-First Lady because of a personal request from the President. A comic tug-of-wills battle between the pair follows. From playing golf in the middle of winter to trips to the opera and periodic escapes in Secret Service cars, Chesnic is constantly chasing after McLaine, trying to keep her under control. Things take a more dramatic turn when she is kidnapped, and Chesnic has to battle with the FBI to rescue her.

Guarding Tess was an offbeat drama disguised as a comedy. With a short haircut and sporting a suit and tie combination, Nic played his straightest role yet. He's a comic foil for McLaine's eccentricities. He manages to put on a great Buster Keaton-style 'stone face' expression, but overall he didn't seem suited to either suits or this subdued part.

'I had wanted to really do something light, something to prove I could do comedy,' Nic said of *Guarding Tess*, probably the least interesting film in his career.

Out of his depth in Red Rock West, *Nic Cage co-starred with the late character actor J. T. Walsh.*

'Then, I did three. I never want to do the same type thing in a row. I like to keep people guessing, particularly myself.'

The 'cop movie' that *Honeymoon In Vegas* director Andrew Bergman had mentioned to Nic turned out to be *It Could Happen To You*, a delightful romantic comedy about a warm-at-heart cop who doesn't have enough money to give a waitress a tip, so offers to split any winnings from a lottery ticket with her. Nic played the laid-back cop, and Bridget Fonda the waitress. When their numbers come up, Nic sets out to honour his promise, only to run into opposition from his screeching wife, played to perfection by Rosie Perez with what Nic called 'sort of the American grate voice'.

Bergman based his film on a true story about a cop who really had been short of a tip and offered to share any lottery winnings with the waitress in his local coffee shop. Shooting began on the film under the working title of *Cop Gives Waitress $2 Million Tip!*, later shortened to *Cop Tips Waitress $2 Million*, before the more ordinary sounding *It Could Happen To You*.

The film was a very light comedy, a character piece, and Nic saw much of veteran actor James Stewart in the character of Charlie Lang. It was the kind of nice-guy role Stewart might have tackled back in the forties, and that was how Nic decided to do it. 'I was nervous that people were going to slam me for that,' he said of his decision. 'Everyone knows that imitation is the worst thing you can do in acting. I'm

Guarding Tess proves to be a tough task for Agent Doug Chesnic (Cage). Nic enjoyed the chance to co-star with veteran Shirley McLaine.

not sure that's true – I've always felt that we have a little bit of good and bad in us, that's what makes us complicated. But Charlie was good, good, good. I wanted to play him a little larger than life. Naturalism is a style that can be really effective, but it can be really boring.'

Nic had tried the naturalistic, toned-down approach to comedy in *Guarding Tess* without great success. Here was a chance to return to what he did best – bring his own heightened performance to distinguish an otherwise ordinary character. It was the reason Andrew Bergman wanted to work with his *Honeymoon In Vegas* star again. 'He makes ordinary guys interesting,' confirmed Bergman. 'There's nothing white bread about anything he does. There's something so unadorned about the way he says "A promise is a promise" in that movie, it just gives you goose bumps.'

The James Stewart impersonation seemed to be working – it gave Nic a clear focus for his character and director Bergman seemed to approve. Nic claims that during filming Bergman would urge him to give the part 'more Jimmy, more Jimmy'. Nic was happy to oblige: 'It was the Jimmy Stewart movie. I'm such a huge admirer – he was such an American icon – that I'd hesitate to say I was impersonating him. It was really more of a tip of the hat, a kind of homage. I do think he had what seemed to be a pure American innocence, which trembled on the screen in a way that gave people hope. There isn't a lot of that in movies today. I'd done so many subversive, twisted characters on the darker side of things that it had been time to lighten up.'

The film was shot on over 100 locations throughout New York City, the coffee shop being just around the corner from the World Trade Center. When released in

February 1995, it won Nic a series of winning reviews. The *San Francisco Chronicle* said: 'the latest attempt to do a Frank Capra-style film in the nineties . . . has two things going for it: Nicolas Cage and Bridget Fonda'. Cage fan Roger Ebert wrote in the *Chicago Sun-Times* that 'Cage has a certain gentleness that brings out nice soft smiles on Fonda's face.'

Although he was to play in one more comedy before returning to meatier, more dramatic roles, Nic rightly doesn't regard *Trapped In Paradise* as one of his better movies. Like *Amos And Andrew* and *Deadfall*, it must have looked like a good idea on paper, but the finished film turned out to be huge disappointment for him.

An ensemble comedy which began shooting under the title *It Happened In Paradise*, the movie teamed Nic up with TV comedians Jon Lovitz and Dana Carvey, the latter of whom had appeared in a bit part alongside Cage in *Racing With The Moon* over a decade before in 1984, but was now better known as one of the stars of the *Wayne's World* movies. Nic played Bill Firpo, one of three brothers who team up to rob a small town bank on Christmas Eve, but then find they can't escape the town. Nic was mistakenly cast as the straight man against Lovitz and Carvey's irritating giggling imbeciles, and although there are flashes of those Cage trademark moments, his frustrations at the limitations of his role seem to come through in his performance.

For a comedy film, *Trapped In Paradise* was overlong and not very funny. The three central characters are not particularly likeable and their plan to rob the bank in

Short of a tip for a waitress (Bridget Fonda), Nic offers to share his prize if his lottery ticket wins in It Could Happen To You.

the perfect town of Paradise in Pennsylvania is half-hearted at best. Throw in the town's too-good-to-be-true residents, assorted dumb cops, escaped mobsters after the cash and attempts to flee the town by car, bus, boat and horse and sleigh, and the ridiculous convolutions are clear. When the three Firpo brothers take refuge with the bank manager, his family and lodger (*Twin Peaks*' Mädchen Amick), Bill Firpo notes: 'I just robbed these people, I don't want to get to know them.' But get to know them he does and his knowledge leads to a change of heart. He returns the money and the townsfolk conspire to save the ill-fated trio from the FBI. At the end, Nic's character remains trapped in the town, in Paradise.

After *Trapped In Paradise* Nic felt a need to return to his roots. He had the mainstream success he'd wanted now, as well as a strong and growing fan following. He felt the urge to play a darker character once again, to challenge himself and challenge his audiences to stick with him. The result was Little Junior Brown in *Kiss Of Death*.

Kiss Of Death was the ideal vehicle. The film was a remake of a 1947 original which had featured Victor Mature as an ex-con who just can't escape the bent life, and Richard Widmark, who stole the acting honours, as a bloodthirsty killer. Director Henry Hathaway had approached the gripping – and for the time, shocking – material with an almost clinical, documentary approach, making the immorality of the characters all that more chilling.

Acclaimed director Barbet Schroeder was making the new version, and had signed up TV star David Caruso to play the leading role of the ex-con drawn back into his old ways by threats against his wife and children. Caruso had created a stir when he abandoned his leading role in the hit cop show *NYPD Blue* after just one season to pursue a career in the movies. *Kiss Of Death* was his first major role since that decision, although he'd previously had a large part opposite Robert DeNiro in *Mad Dog And Glory*.

Nic was being tapped for Little Junior Brown, the Richard Widmark role. The over-the-top nastiness of the part was right up his street, taking him back to his pre-nice guy comedy roles. His only worry was being asked to act in support of newcomer Caruso. By 1994–5 Cage's asking price was up to $4 million per film, which didn't put him in the Mel Gibson, Harrison Ford or Tom Cruise league, but was still a tidy sum. 'My agent said, "You can't support David Caruso in a movie," but I really wanted to play the part. I had to get back to wearing my black clothes. I thought, why not – David's a good actor and I can support him.'

Nic plunged into the part with a vengeance, dredging up all his method acting tricks and spending two hours per day for two months on a body-building regime. He augmented this with a dietary programme encompassing eight meals a day backed up by protein drinks. His aim was to bulk up physically so as to capture the menacing nature of Little Junior Brown.

The screenwriter who brought Cage's character and Caruso's Jimmy Kilmartin to life was Richard Price, best known for a series of novellas as well as the screenplays for *The Color Of Money* (directed by Martin Scorsese, for which Price won an Academy Award nomination), *Sea Of Love* and *Mad Dog And Glory*. Director Barbet

When his lottery ticket wins Nic keeps his promise to the waitress, much to the annoyance of his wife, played by Rosie Perez (right).

Schroeder's most recent work had included the urban thriller *Single White Female*, starring Bridget Fonda and Jennifer Jason Leigh; *Reversal Of Fortune*, for which Schroeder won Academy Award and Golden Globe nominations as Best Director in 1990; and *Barfly*, based on the writings of the late Charles Bukowski.

Price's latest screenplay held numerous attractions for Schroeder. 'I was fascinated by the script's documentary-like depiction of New York's criminal underworld and of the police and justice system,' he said, pleased to see that at least in atmosphere the film could be faithful to the original. 'The first draft had very little to do with the 1947 movie. By the time we started shooting, only the title and one plot point remained. Also the material had, like other Price works, a very strong New York flavour. The movie could only be made in New York and, more precisely, in Queens.'

For David Caruso, the dilemmas faced by his character in walking the line between the law and the criminal underworld were at the heart of the film. 'Jimmy is in the ultimate version of a rock and a hard place,' said Caruso. 'He's forced to rise to a life-and-death challenge with the various and nefarious characters with whom he is confronted; in the mix of all that, he's trying to remain constant with his own code of honor.'

Little Junior Brown was one of the principal figures who put Jimmy to the test. Despite the character's prominence in the underworld, Nic saw the criminal overlord as much more than a stereotype. 'Even though Little Junior is a very scary and very powerful human being, I don't think that he is evil,' he explained. 'He's doing what he feels he has to do to survive in the urban jungle.'

Nic was keen to personalise him, by bringing something of himself, something out of his own life to the role. His son Weston had been suffering from asthma, a

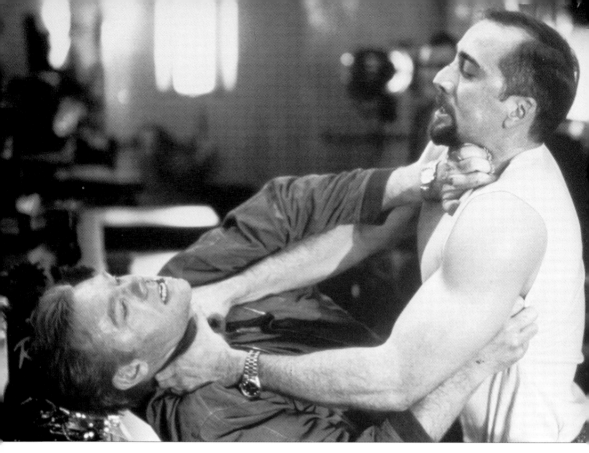

David Caruso co-starred with Nic Cage (as mobster Little Junior Brown) in the violent thriller Kiss Of Death.

condition which co-incidentally had been written into the script for Little Junior Brown. He observed Weston closely, picking up how he used his inhaler, absorbing something of what it means to be suffering from asthma, and brought his observations to bear on his performance.

The research paid off. The reviews that greeted the release of *Kiss Of Death* in May 1995 were mixed, but most praised Nic's performance, while criticising that of Caruso. *Time* Magazine stated that 'hypnotic psychopathy is never in short supply when Cage is aslither'. *USA Today* dubbed Cage's character as 'a scary goateed dude who bench-presses strippers in a Queens, N.Y., joint called Baby Cakes', while *Entertainment Weekly* noted that Nic 'goateed and obscenely pumped up, makes this homicidal creep dense and quick at the same time. He registers only what's directly in front of him, yet he hones in on that with a bullet-like swiftness. It's a mesmerising performance, comic but never just comic.'

Coming back to playing a nasty character, Nic discovered that *Kiss Of Death* had a profound effect on him – something he put down to the fact that he now had a four-year-old son to consider. 'I realised on *Kiss Of Death* that by the end of the day I was nauseous with it – threatening one guy with a cigarette or punching somebody to death. I just thought, I don't want to go there any more. I didn't want to go to that shitty little corner of my mind where I could actually see myself contemplating this behaviour.' It was an echo of his onetime fear that he might have turned to crime in his teenage years if he had not become absorbed by acting.

Cage had brought all the anger and passion that he knew as a teenager to the role. He'd done the physical preparation for the part, but he hadn't been prepared for the mental effect the role of an unredeemed thug would have on him. As a father, he had changed. 'I'd rather be playing fire truck with my son,' he realised when confronted with the dark depths of Little Junior Brown. He was still coping with the 'extreme elation and worry that comes with fatherhood' and it was to colour the direction his career would take from here.

Although by the time *Kiss Of Death* was released in 1995 Cage had moved onto other roles, he was still focusing on the by then five-year-old Weston. 'Suddenly, I realised I live for someone other than myself. I tend to be at times more sensitive than a lot of fathers. I worry a lot. I'm always concerned that Weston is OK – phoning to make sure he's come home, that sort of Jewish parent/Italian parent stuff,' he said, living up to his third-generation Italian American heritage.

Before Nic could embark on the next stage of his career, he had domestic issues to deal with. His up-and-down two year relationship with Kristen Zang was drawing to a close. The pair seemed to be spending more time apart than together, while Nic was also spending a lot of his time with Christina Fulton and Weston, which did not please Kristen. She was significantly younger than him, at an age when all she really wanted to do was enjoy herself, but since he'd become a father, Nic was taking his responsibilities more seriously and the party-hearty lifestyle has ceased to be an attraction. 'I've slowed down,' he admitted. 'I'm a worrywart now.'

The incompatibility in their lifestyles and Nic's suspicion that Kristen was not being entirely faithful to him were at the root of their break-up. Cage had been through this several times before, but he'd foreseen this one, unlike in the past. That didn't make their parting any easier. 'The split up was difficult,' said Cage, who'd denied rumours that he and Zang had been engaged at one point. 'It had been a stormy relationship, but it was also a sweet relationship. We just weren't right for each other. I was a lot older than she was. I had to get up early and she liked to sleep like you do when you're eighteen. She wanted to go to night-clubs. There was a sadness when we had to split up and that sadness went into *Leaving Las Vegas*, because the break-up came at around the same time. A lot of the times I was saying "I love you," I was just heartbroken.'

Nic retreated to his gothic castle high in the Hollywood Hills to lick his emotional wounds and to begin preparation for his next film: Mike Figgis's *Leaving Las Vegas*, a low-budget independent movie which would bring him his greatest acting challenge and his greatest acclaim.

8. Hidden Treasure

WHILE FILMING *TRAPPED IN PARADISE* in the snowy wastes of Canada, Nic Cage had received a script which had captured his imagination. 'It seemed the answer to all my prayers. I was fed up with the movies I was making and it gave me an opportunity to go back to a darker corner of my mind. The script astounded me. I was crying when I finished reading it. It is more than anything a story of unconditional love. It was definitely one of the coolest relationships I'd ever read in a screenplay.'

The author of the screenplay was British writer-director Mike Figgis. He had begun his career in music and theatre in Britain, before directing the Newcastle-set thriller *Stormy Monday* in 1988. Although not well regarded in Britain, the film won Figgis the opportunity to direct an American police corruption thriller *Internal Affairs*, with Richard Gere and Andy Garcia. The success of that movie gave him the chance to produce a personal project, the dark, compelling and wildly underrated *Liebestraum*, a 1991 mystery-thriller starring Kevin Anderson, Bill Pullman and Kim Novak. The film bombed, knocking Figgis off the list of hot Hollywood directors.

His comeback venture was a studio project called *Mr Jones* about an affair between a manic depressive (also played by Richard Gere) and his psychiatrist (Lena Olin). Figgis ran into problems with studio executives who worried about the dark nature of some of the material and wondered out loud whether it would be OK to make Gere's character only manic and lose the depressive bit. This interference provoked Figgis into hitting out at the Hollywood system, resulting in many 'he'll never work in this town again' type comments. He had reached the lowest point in his career so far, and needed a new project to both get him working again and to rehabilitate his image with the Hollywood money men.

'I think I've got an image as a trouble maker,' he admitted. 'It's not like I'm declaring war on Hollywood. What's the point? It's like trying to declare war on the sea. It comes and goes.' His next job was another studio picture – an updating of *The Browning Version* for Paramount. It served to get him working again, but he found himself clashing with fellow British director Ridley Scott who was acting as producer

on the film. 'He's a film-maker with a very strong point of view – not necessarily the same as my point of view,' Figgis said of Scott. Again, Figgis was on the verge of falling out with Hollywood – and then he came across a little-known novel by John O'Brien called *Leaving Las Vegas*. 'I remember saying that it was a great book and I really wanted to make it, but I knew we didn't have a hope in hell of raising the money.'

John O'Brien's semi-autobiographical novel told the bleak tale of the final weeks in the life of Ben, an alcoholic screenwriter who has reached the end of his tether. Dumped by his agent, Ben decides to move to Las Vegas to drink himself to death. There he gets briefly distracted from his aim of self-destruction when he meets Sera, a Vegas prostitute whose life has been even harder than his. It was clearly not the stuff of the million-dollar special-effects Hollywood blockbuster.

The material had a strong hold on Figgis and he knew it would be a struggle to capture on film what O'Brien had achieved on the page. 'It's incredibly romantic and that appealed to me enormously. I felt that O'Brien had cleverly submerged his romanticism, almost out of toughness, almost as if he were saying, "I'm not gonna wear my heart on my sleeve, but it will be visible from time-to-time."' The strength of the material, though, gave Figgis an approach to take to the film he wanted to make. 'The story's so tough that I knew the film would only hang together if we were bold in the same way. It's like, all right, we're gonna be bold – let's cast Nicolas Cage. That was a statement of intent.'

Nic was ready to do the film as soon as he'd finished reading the screenplay, but Mike Figgis faced the difficult task of raising the money first, allowing Nic to go on and make *Kiss Of Death* and a guest appearance in the TV show *Hi-Octane* in the meantime. Figgis was unsure how financiers would react to the project he was putting forward so decided to keep things simple. 'I knew that the only way to make it would be to keep the budget so low that it wouldn't be an embarrassment to anyone if the film wasn't a success.' But he didn't even get that far, as every studio in Hollywood rejected the source material as too bleak. Returning to Europe in his quest for finance, Figgis then persuaded French company Lumière to put up the paltry (in Hollywood terms) $3.5 million he required, allowing him to make the film in 1994.

Working within these strict financial limitations, Figgis saw *Leaving Las Vegas* as a way of achieving some of his own technical ambitions while retaining his anti-Hollywood credentials. 'I had always wanted to shoot a feature on Super-16mm film. I wanted that raw feel, shooting on the lam, doing everything myself.' This down-and-dirty approach suited the subject matter, but it was as much a result of the lack of money and circumstances of the film's production as it was an artistic statement from Figgis. 'I laid down certain ground rules for myself, because of the whole studio experience. I saw it as a turning point. I was really dissatisfied with film-making; the way things were going. I wanted to go back to a sort of funkier way of working, so I told myself I would restrict the budget – that includes everybody, Nicolas, me, the lot. Everybody's doing it for scale, literally.'

Far from demanding his usual $4 million for the film, Nic was so desperate to play this off-the-beaten-track, non-Hollywood part that he would have worked for nothing, let alone the $240,000 actors' union scale minimum that the production offered. 'I would never have been able to make *Leaving Las Vegas* if I hadn't had

some commercial success before that,' he admitted. 'If I hadn't had some semblance of a career I never would have had enough money to do that film. Part of my plan has been to constantly change and do the unexpected. I've always believed that these unexpected hidden treasures, like *Leaving Las Vegas*, will keep coming my way. I did it because it was a great role. I did it because it was different.'

Figgis saw in Nic exactly what he felt was needed for the role of Ben. He felt Nic's brand of 'don't care' recklessness was 'totally appropriate. Then I discovered that he's actually the most brilliant actor I've ever worked with. He's awesome. He can do anything.'

First Nic had to get out of shape to play the part of Ben: 'I found myself in circumstances where I had to shift gears from being this kick-ass gorilla of a man [for *Kiss Of Death*] to playing a weak man who was self-destructive. There was not a whole lot of time to lose the muscle mass I gained. So, I found myself eating junk food and making myself into a flabby guy that felt lousy all the time. I ate a lot of candy and quarter-pounders with cheese.'

Nic's old preparation techniques returned with a vengeance. 'The most impressive thing is the extent and depth of his preparation,' Figgis said of him. Nic was determined to get to the heart of the character, to find out how he ticks, so as to be able to play the role as naturally as possible. It led to an obsession with details which would probably pass most movie-goers by. For example, late one evening Nic called Figgis at home to ask why the director had specified that Ben, a washed-up movie writer, would drive a Jaguar. He claimed that Ben would be behind the wheel of a black BMW, just like every other player in Hollywood. Figgis agreed. Nic continued his trawl through the script, querying 'the clothes, the words, everything,' according to Figgis.

'He's something of an outsider in his family, and I don't think he's ever completely gotten over some of the hurts,' Figgis felt. 'But for an artist, that pain and insecurity is worth its weight in gold. It gives Nic acute powers of observation.'

Nic plunged into the world of the alcoholic, aiming to discover about the physical side of alcoholism, to learn from watching hospital patients enduring the delirium terrors and drawing from the way John O'Brien described his convulsing stomach in the book. While he drew back from trying to become an alcoholic, he, along with Mike Figgis, his co-star Elizabeth Shue and his manager Gerry Harrington, set out on a pub crawl – all in the interest of research. 'I spoke with some drunks and asked questions about their addiction, and met with people from programmes that work with alcoholics,' he reported.

Nic even made a home video tape of himself getting drunk on gin and talking to the camera. His aim was to study the footage to see how he spoke when drunk so when it came to acting he could accurately recreate his own slurs. When he was finished, he made sure he personally erased the tape in case it should fall into the 'wrong hands'. He also watched movies that featured other drunks: 'I studied all the great performances of alcoholics in the past – Ray Milland in *The Lost Weekend*, Jack Lemmon in *Days Of Wine And Roses* and especially Dudley Moore in *Arthur* . . . I was also greatly impressed by Dudley. *Arthur* is not a great movie, but Dudley captured the feeling of a drunk who thinks he's being charming, when he's, really, just being drunk. Dudley was the only one who experimented with a very true thing – that drunks get louder. I wanted to get that.'

Nic even went off to Ireland for a two-week Guinness-sampling session with his friend songwriter Phil Roy. The pair travelled round in a hired car, checking out the joys of Irish pubs, with Nic especially studying the easy charm displayed by some of the drinkers. He was after 'some essence, some soul, in the land of great writers and drinkers'.

'Basically,' recalled Roy, 'we did Ireland by night.' At one point on the trek, the pair stopped to pick up the daughter of some aristocrats who then joined them for three days. When she told them about a supposedly haunted castle near Galway, Nic got excited. 'We gotta go, man. We gotta go,' he exclaimed, before setting off for the castle. Leap Castle, ancestral home of the O'Carrolls, welcomed their visitors with tales of a supposedly smelly ghoul. Staying up all night in a room lit only by a candle, Nic and Roy were disappointed not to be visited by the resident spook. 'This,' remembered Roy, 'was just a night with Nic.'

Although Nic took his fair share of drinks in preparation for the part he claimed not to have a problem himself, despite his early days in Hollywood on the tiles with the likes of Sean Penn and Jim Carrey. 'I drink socially,' he said. 'I drink with my friends on occasion. It's not something that's gotten in the way of my life.' And despite its obviously cautionary subject matter, Cage didn't want *Leaving Las Vegas* to be seen as a 'message' film. 'I can't get on that high horse and say "This is what happens to you when you drink alcohol." Some people don't know moderation. They don't want to know. You can't say a glass of red wine is going to kill you or give you a problem. I didn't expect it would even be released. I thought it would be too dark.'

Back in Los Angeles, he rented out several suites of the Chateau Marmont on Sunset Strip at his own expense so that he and Elizabeth Shue, who played Sera, could rehearse the film in depth, as the low budget would not allow them the time in the compact four-week location shoot. Cage had never worked with Shue, but he was aware of her from lightweight films like *Adventures In Baby-sitting* and *Cocktail*. He was nervous about his own abilities to play the part of Ben, but that was compounded by his doubts about whether Shue could handle the equally demanding role of Sera. The rehearsals would be a chance for him to find out.

'I didn't know her work very well,' he admitted. 'There was nothing in it to suggest this depth.' Nic knew he and Shue had to work on developing a chemistry between them that would come across on the movie screen. In fact, he found that working with her came naturally after all: 'She's mesmerising because she is so wholesome in appearance. And what happens is so devastating. I was particularly worried about the love story. Elisabeth Shue and I didn't know each other at all before, and it was a pure story about unconditional love, two people who trusted each other completely.'

Although the rehearsal period was useful – if only for Cage and Shue to get to know each other – the star was wary of relying on it too much in how he would play the part, preferring the freewheeling spontaneity of the shoot. 'Too much rehearsal can ruin a performance,' he said. 'That's one thing I liked about *Leaving Las Vegas*. It was done so quickly, and with that tiny, 16mm camera. That camera is wonderful for actors. You hardly know it's there.'

Two weeks into pre-production on the film, the cast and crew were met with devastating news. John O'Brien had killed himself. 'It stopped me in my tracks,' said a stunned Mike Figgis. 'You can't romanticise a situation where the creator has done what he said he was going to do in the book. I suddenly realised it was serious, not a whim or a fantasy.'

O'Brien had grown up in a working-class neighbourhood of Cleveland, before marrying Lisa Kirkwood and moving to Los Angeles. An aspiring writer, he had reacted to the seemingly endless series of rejection slips by becoming addicted to alcohol. By the time he achieved some measure of success with the publication of *Leaving Las Vegas* by Watermark Press, a small Kansas company, and the optioning of the movie rights by Mike Figgis, he couldn't stop himself drinking. The book seemed to become a manifesto for his life and death. While writing a second book – *The Assault On Tony's*, published after his death in 1997 – O'Brien was on the verge of losing his job at a Hollywood coffee house and his wife into the bargain.

In April 1994, O'Brien's father was informed that the author had been admitted to the Brotman Medical Centre in Los Angeles after he'd been beaten up in the street. He was told that such were the nature of his son's injuries that if he didn't stop drinking immediately he would certainly die. According to Bill O'Brien, John was adamant: 'No one is going to tell me I'm going to stop drinking.' It was a line Nicolas Cage would later use in the film. Three weeks later the 33-year-old was dead, but not from alcohol. He'd shot himself in the head.

John O'Brien's death was a jolt not only for Mike Figgis, but for Nic too, who'd be – to all intents and purposes – playing a version of him in the film. 'I really felt the weight of playing a dead man's suicide note,' he said of the traumatic four-week shoot for the film in Nevada that September. 'Ben is self-destructive and the hard thing to do was to manifest the physical deterioration of an alcoholic to that acute point. I guess John O'Brien had a very sad life. One day his family all came to the set – it was a kind of a spooky day. I was wearing the exact same watch that John wore . . .'

Nic had some personal investment in the role, too, as it allowed him finally to come to terms with the death of Francis Ford Coppola's son Gian-Carlo, who'd died in a boating accident in 1986. 'Maybe by some definition my cousin's death impacted on my decision to do the movie, although it's an entirely different situation. It got me thinking about death at an early age.'

Other personal issues fed into Cage's performance – not the least of which was his recent break-up with Kristen Zang. 'I was going through my own private wringer with the end of the relationship with Kristen. In a lot of ways that fuelled the performance. She and I were not happy at that point and it just went right into the character.'

Arriving at the Gold River Resort in Laughlin, Nevada in September 1994, Nic

Cage took his preparations for Leaving Las Vegas *seriously, even videotaping himself drunk as part of his research.*

made a big impact on the hotel staff. They expected to have to indulge a rising Hollywood star's every whim – they didn't expect to be dealing with suicidal alcoholic Ben Sanderson. That's how Nic checked in – as movie character Ben, not actor Nic Cage, then phoned the front desk to order up a bottle of vodka and some cranberry juice. 'He was really bizarre,' said casino manager Brad Overfield of the hotel's maverick guest. 'A lot of people thought he had to be drunk or on drugs because he was so intense.'

It was all just part of Nic's method of dumping Nicolas Coppola/Cage and becoming Ben Sanderson. Despite what the hotel staff may have thought and Mike Figgis might have feared, Nic didn't totally immerse himself in the role. As with *Kiss Of Death*, he found himself drawing on his son Weston for inspiration. He based some of his character on the 'beauty and fragility' of the then four-year-old Weston. He readily admitted that if he hadn't gone through the 'extremes of worry and elation' that had come with fatherhood, he would have found it much more difficult to do justice to the role. 'When I was doing Ben, I asked myself, "What is most heartbreaking?" The behaviour of a four-year-old boy . . .'

The 28-day low-budget shoot was intense for all involved, not least for Elizabeth Shue. 'The first day we sat down and had about six therapy sessions . . . it was an incredible experience, to know that I knew who this person was in therapy emotionally, and it made me feel really strong about going into the movie . . .'

Nic had a definite approach in mind to bringing Ben Sanderson to life. 'I wanted Ben to be a kind of study in crumbled elegance – at one time probably the life of the party. A real social star with a great way with words, real command of the language, and a sense of style – the watch he wears, the way he dresses. And he's gone to the point where it's all starting to decay.'

Nic was as inventive as ever when it came to the way to shoot specific scenes. According to Elizabeth Shue, it was his idea to sing a made-up song during Ben's first, unsuccessful attempt at oral sex. 'I go to change in the bathroom for this scene,' recalled Shue, 'and he was out there singing this Batmobile song he'd made up. It was just so odd. I kept laughing and he really got my attention. He drew me in and kept me looking honest.'

Throwing in the song was 'a pivotal moment,' according to Mike Figgis, because 'it says [this character has] enough innate grace and humility that sex is not his sole agenda. And consequently made it a great sex scene.'

However Nic's next suggestion did not go down so well with his director. It was, according to Figgis, the only time during the month of shooting that they clashed. When filming the scene where Ben arrives at Sera's apartment, suffering after a bar brawl, Nic chose to insert some lines of his own devising. 'I was not quite prepared for him to say he felt "like the kling-klang king of the rim-ram room," which wasn't in the script,' recalled Figgis. 'So I shouted as we rolled for the next take, "Good luck with the improvisation." Well, Nic got a look and said, "Oh, okay, I'll do a real straight one for ya then." I had made the mistake of thinking it was arbitrary, when in fact he'd worked it all out very carefully. He's still very sensitive about the perception that he's wacky, because his performance isn't that. It's all hard work. Nothing in it is arbitrary.'

Elizabeth Shue was surprised how much input Nic had into his lines, and how much leeway he was given by the director. 'You can't believe how many lines in the movie are Nic's,' she said, 'from "I'm a prickly pear" to the "kling-klang king". I love it that there are moments in film history where there is one person who can play a part and one person only.' His success with rewriting his dialogue and thinking up bits of business to sneak into this movie would encourage him further in his next few movies – a development which brought him praise from some directors, but also anger from of some of the writers.

For Mike Figgis, the whole process, despite (or because of) the financial limitations, was like no other film he'd ever worked on. 'This is the strongest film-making experience I've ever had,' he claimed, 'and the best performances I've ever gotten out of any actors. I think the script is really good because the book was good. I think it's a fantastic story. The dialogue is incredible and Cage is a kind of phenomenon. I think he's surprised himself in this. Certainly, he surprised me.'

Shooting was something of an adventure as Figgis couldn't afford the necessary permits to film on location in Las Vegas, so he undertook a type of guerrilla film-making, co-opting his leading actors. 'The city took exception to the script,' noted the director. 'No one would give us an interior to shoot in and we had to use the Laughlin, which is about an hour away from Las Vegas. The Vegas police also have the right to ban you from filming on the streets. We didn't have permission to stop the traffic, so the actors had to compete with the real world – no bad thing from time-to-time.'

Another limitation on the film was the need to record the sound live on location rather than overdubbing (looping) later as most big-budget movies would do. 'We're going with it,' said Figgis, faced with the need to record his soundtrack live. 'By using the long lens we can get close-miked. The sound will be a problem, for sure, but I'm not going to loop, so we're going to have to live with it.' Again, it was a case of a production expediency suiting the atmosphere the film needed and the gritty nature of the material.

For Nic, Shue and Figgis, shooting on the run, quickly and with the minimum of fuss was the opposite of most Hollywood films. They threw themselves into the experience, none more so than Figgis, who relished the return to his low-budget roots. 'I didn't want to intrude on the character's lives,' he said of his camera technique. 'I think that the over-sophistication of film technique has resulted in a psychological situation where the audience just accept that they're being manipulated all the time.'

Figgis worked very closely with Nic on his performance, making sure that they shared the same approach to the material and making sure that Nic's extremes of research and method obsession didn't obscure the heart of the film. 'I didn't want it to cross the line where it freaks people out,' Nic noted of his own approach. 'I didn't want to get to the point where they say, "Oh we don't have to see that, I don't want to see that." I wanted it to be accessible to people because I think that the love story is very profound.'

Elizabeth Shue found herself somewhat in awe of her co-star, aware of his reputation for scene-stealing and meticulous preparation for a role. 'I was nervous to work with Nic, I think,' she admitted. 'I was nervous only in that I wouldn't – that we wouldn't be equal in some ways. I have so much respect for him. I've watched all of his work and I find him so incredible as an actor.'

Nic was only too aware that he was acting out his character's final days. Rather than come at it as a depressing time, Cage felt that an attitude of freedom was more appropriate. 'It was like he's got 45 days left, let's make it a roller coaster and let's do everything, because he's not afraid of death. And a man who isn't afraid to die can really do anything. He can sing while getting a blow job. He can do whatever he wants . . . Here is a man who is going down the river, but he's not grabbing for the branches so there's no struggle or strain. He's completely loose and somewhat liberated. He's not afraid of death, and a man who isn't afraid to die can really do anything. He's free.'

However, the death scene itself was something of a daunting moment for the actor, aware that the burden of the film's future success or failure was lying heavily on his shoulders. 'In the death scene, I really wanted Ben to die saying, "Wow". 'When you see death in films, it's always portrayed as being painful and lonely. But we don't know, it could be anything – it could be a roller coaster ride. I wanted it to be the beginning of a trip. Ben's in pain, but he's seeing something. I didn't want to make a movie about alcoholism. It was a love story about these two people.'

Consistent with this view, Nic believed that, despite the sordid nature of some of the

Nic described Leaving Las Vegas *as 'a pure story of unconditional love, two people who trusted each other completely'.*

story, *Leaving Las Vegas* had about it something of a redemptive quality: 'If he'd never been a drunk, he'd never have met his true love,' said Cage of his character. 'Yeah, he wrecks himself but at the same time, he has an experience not everyone gets in a whole lifetime.'

Mike Figgis was pleasantly surprised by the work done by both Elizabeth Shue and Nic, especially as neither had been the obvious choices for the roles. 'They are way, way beyond my expectation of how good they'd be. I always thought they'd be good, but you know, you go on your instinct and you don't know how your instinct is going to pan out . . . I'm ecstatic.'

Between October and December 1995, Mike Figgis and the film's leading actors underwent a series of screenings and interview sessions to promote *Leaving Las Vegas* in major American cities. It was a process none of the participants particularly enjoyed, despite their unshakeable belief in the film. Figgis, in particular, recorded his disenchantment with the process in a diary he kept of the period.

Flying from industry, press and public preview screenings in Los Angeles, Seattle, San Francisco and San Diego, he found it hard to gauge the reaction to the movie. He knew there might be some controversy over the alcoholism depicted in the film. 'We were warned after an early screening that we might get some flak from Alcoholics Anonymous, but I don't think anyone would want to become an alcoholic after seeing the film. And we've had no backlash from the AA.'

It was only when he returned to Los Angeles in the middle of October that the director began to get an inkling of what was to come. On what might have been an

'They are way beyond my expectation of how good they'd be,' said director Mike Figgis of Elizabeth Shue and Nic Cage.

unlucky Friday the 13th October 1995, he noted, 'The response is starting to show. Robert Newman (my American agent) is playing it cool and we'll just see how it pans out.' Two days later he candidly admitted: 'I'm quietly becoming excited.'

Further screenings took place, in New York, Boston and Chicago during the rest of October. At the end of the month, Figgis was back in Los Angeles to host an American Film Institute tribute to Nicolas Cage and to be around for the opening of *Leaving Las Vegas,* in only six cities initially. The film took over $200,000 in its first week, with the box office climbing 50 per cent the following week – an usual event for a limited-release art house film. Figgis noted in his diary: 'This is very rare and will probably encourage United Artists to go wider with the release.'

A London Film Festival screening followed in early November, prior to the UK release of the film early in January 1996. Between November and January, the American success of the film continued to grow, with a series of cracking reviews and an honour list of award nominations for the film, director and the cast. *Rolling Stone* picked the film as one of their favourites of the year, while the National Board of Review (made up of movie critics) awarded the Best Actor nod to Nicolas Cage. For Figgis the possibilities of greater glory loomed: 'Oscars suddenly seem possible,' he noted in his diary, 'and against my better judgement I find myself becoming excited and insomniac.' His hopes were further buoyed by the New York Critics awarding *Leaving Las Vegas* Best Film and Nicolas Cage Best Actor. 'Everyone is high with Oscar fever,' wrote Figgis, 'and the film will now go wider and make more money.'

The reviews of the film and of the leading performances were even more heartwarming for Figgis and his two stars. 'This harrowing story of love without judgement, of acceptance without explanation, is straight, no-chaser adult entertainment, seen through a haze of dizzying intoxication and driven by powerful performances,' noted Stephen Saban in *Details* magazine. Reviewers were falling over themselves to praise the film: 'The two Oscar-calibre performances by Nicolas Cage and the smashing Elisabeth Shue are in a class by themselves,' said Rex Reed in the *New York Observer*, while 'Against all odds, *Leaving Las Vegas* is the most unabashedly romantic love story released so far this year,' was the judgement of J. Hoberman in *Premiere* magazine.

More interestingly, critics found themselves having to revise their opinions of Nicolas Cage. 'I have not always believed in Nicolas Cage,' admitted David Thomson in *Los Angeles* magazine, publicly rewriting his opinion of the actor. 'He has a tendency to make gestures toward a level of knowledge that is lacking. As Ben, he is tender, foolish, weak, kind – it is the guy from *Moonstruck* turned into a disaster by life. If there's a truer screen drunk around, I don't know if I could stand it. He is extraordinary.'

Others were more succinct in their unstinting praise for Cage. 'Cage has simply never been better,' said David Bartholomew in *Film Journal*, while Peter Travers in *Rolling Stone* noted: 'Cage gives a blazing performance that cuts through Ben's alcoholic haze to reveal a startling sweetness and clarity.'

Nic attended the Toronto International Film Festival six weeks before the film opened in the United States. He and Patricia Arquette (whom he'd married by that time) sat through the screening at the Uptown Theater. Cage gripped Arquette's hand during the film's more harrowing scenes, surveying the audience in the theatre, trying to guess their response. 'I was happy,' he said. 'It was the first time I'd seen it with a live audience. There was laughter in places I hadn't expected. The subject matter is kind of dark. It's like with drunks. Sometimes they say something incredibly funny, then they do something depressing. My character knows he's going to die. He's liberated. A guy like that is sometimes cheery, sometimes funny.'

At the end of the screening, the film received polite and respectful applause, before the audience quietly filed out of the cinema. It wasn't the kind of film to generate whoops and hollers of appreciation at the end, simply quiet contemplation and appreciation. Things livened up considerably at the post-screening party, however, held at a grunge bar called the Velvet Underground. Nic attended, along with Elizabeth Shue and Mike Figgis, but he was disturbed by speculation that this 'little film', shot in 27 days on 16mm film, would never be properly released.

There were more awards for Nic, with the Los Angeles Critics' Circle awarding the film a clean sweep. Mike Figgis first heard about the success of the film there from its star. 'There was a message from Nic,' he noted in his diary. 'He was trying to be cool about it and making out that the news was bad, and then losing it. It was a clean sweep – best actor, best actress, best film and best director.'

For Nic this praise and the success of the film was a clear vindication of all his work to date. The success of such a 'small, 16mm movie about a very bleak subject,' he said, 'shows that I wasn't crazy all these years, that I had a point.'

9. The Marrying Man

For Nicolas Cage 1995–6 would be a pair of momentous years. The first year started with him just having completed work on *Leaving Las Vegas*, and after the initial limited release in American cinemas late in 1995 both he and Mike Figgis knew they had a surprise hit on their hands. Bigger things happened during this period, with marriage to Patricia Arquette, a career tribute from the American Film Institute, a win at the Oscars, where Nic walked off with the golden statuette for Best Actor, and a Lifetime Achievement Award from the Montreal Film Festival in 1996. For an actor with little in the way of formal training and a determinedly stubborn streak when it came to selecting roles, Nicolas Cage was finally hitting the big time.

Patricia Arquette had admitted, 'When I love someone I love them for years and years.' The same seemed to be true of Nicolas Cage. Since they'd first met in 1987 and engaged in their bizarre courtship, they had kept in close touch, often talking on the phone and playfully teasing each other about their future marriage plans. Since they'd gone their separate ways, Patricia had also split up with Paul Rossi, the musician father of her son, Enzo. 'When I broke up with Enzo's dad, I hated men so much,' she claimed. She reacted by going out clubbing a lot, dressing provocatively, then abusing anyone who declared an attraction to her. 'I was in a bad state of mind,' she admitted. 'I was so angry.'

Meanwhile, Cage had been involved with Christina Fulton, had his son Weston and then split up from Kristen Zang. He too was in a bad state of mind, and the rigours of working on *Leaving Las Vegas* had done nothing to alleviate it. 'I was going through the thing with Kristen. I loved the person and although the relationship wasn't working, I couldn't leave. I knew it wasn't right for me, I knew we were both unhappy. It was like we kept clinging to each other and it had to come to an end.'

Nic thought he had the answer – he certainly had the money to afford it. 'I went into therapy,' he admitted. 'I was loaded with all these feelings. Therapy was helpful and then I started thinking, "Oh, man – they're taking all this good stuff from me." My acting had been my therapy. The work was what saved me.'

During the sessions on the therapist's couch Nic found his thoughts drifting to

Patricia again and again. While he was trying to get over his relationship with Kristen, images of the relationship he so nearly had with Patricia were coming to dominate his thoughts. It had to mean something, he reasoned, so he took a chance on one of those overblown romantic gestures he'd admitted to in the past.

At 2 a.m. one morning Nic decided to return to Canter's, the 24-hour Jewish deli where he and Patricia had first met and she'd drawn up the list of impossible tasks that was to form his romantic quest. In the kind of bizarre coincidence that seemed such a regular feature of Nic's life, Patricia was there that night. 'She was wearing silver pants,' is all Nic claims to remember about their reunion.

Patricia then flew off to Malaysia in order to shoot the film *Beyond Rangoon* for director John Boorman. When she returned to Los Angeles, she'd made some decisions about important aspects of her life. 'I decided when I came back from Malaysia that I was saying "I love you" to one more person in my life. I wanted a greater kind of love, a forever love, and I wasn't going to trade that off because I was afraid of being alone.'

Later Nic called her up with a strange request. 'I hear you have a boyfriend,' he said to her. 'I gotta go away for a week. Please don't get married while I'm gone. I have a bad feeling.' He had discovered some old letters from her, and the spectre of their almost-relationship had continued to haunt his thoughts.

Patricia's reaction to the call surprised her. 'It freaked me out – where my heart went,' she said. 'The truth of us – that haunted me a lot.' She had co-starred in *True Romance* with Christian Slater, and now she was beginning to realise that perhaps that's what was brewing between her and Nicolas Cage.

Two months later, at the start of April, Patricia called Nic. 'Listen, I have to ask you something. Do you want to marry me?' There was something of a surprised silence at the other end of the telephone from Nic, who was reading a comic-book at the time. Patricia recalled later: 'We hadn't been together for eight years. He said "Yeah, OK, I'll do it."' She didn't want such a seemingly half-hearted reaction. 'No, I'm not kidding,' she said. 'No . . . I'm not either,' came the firmer reply from Nic. 'Something inside me just said "Yes",' Nic remembered. The true romance was back on course after an eight-year pause.

Their wedding was impetuous – within a fortnight of Patricia's sudden and unexpected proposal – but it wasn't frivolous. After all, it had taken the pair of them eight years to get to this stage. 'We jumped in a car, ran off, went to a cliff and got married,' she joked about the speed with which the arrangements had been made. They may have been fast, but both she and Nic were serious with it. 'Neither of us have ever been married,' Patricia said. 'Not for lack of people asking us on either side. It's very serious. We both have kids. We would not do something like that in a sort of haphazard way without knowing in the deepest part of us, "This is right".'

Nic was similarly serious in intent, even if he was light hearted about the actual event. He'd previously claimed in a magazine article to be 'a hard-core commitment phobe' and that had been a problem in his previous relationships. He worried about this one too, up until the day of the wedding. 'It was almost like an arranged marriage, where we rushed into it,' he recalled. 'We didn't have a natural courtship, we just did it. It was a romantic gesture to marry as quickly as we did, but it was not a frivolous decision. I was genuinely aware of what it takes to make a marriage successful.'

Patricia was prepared for adverse publicity, and she was upset at allegations that they were entering into a 'Hollywood marriage', a union of convenience that deflected questions about the couple's relationships and sexuality. 'I know the marriage sounds really weird, incredibly abrupt, but we married out of a deep love for each other, not out of sexuality. We hadn't slept together in eight years,' she said.

'There was no question or doubt in my mind,' said Nic. 'This woman was my equal and I was meant to be with her from long ago. We only went out for three weeks and went on with our lives, and had these kind of extreme adventures that always somehow managed to keep us in synch, along with the parallel family connection in that she came from a creative family . . . We're from the same tribe. I was ready to make that official commitment – I knew that it was time.'

Nicolas and Patricia headed up the pacific coastline to a clifftop site just outside the town of Carmel (where Clint Eastwood had once been mayor) for their wedding, on a crisp, if overcast, late April day in 1995. The minister was Kathee McFarland, and she and her husband Donald – the town's former chief of police – acted as witnesses to the union. This was no big media event, no overblown Hollywood marriage with photographers crowding around, hundreds of celebrity guests and helicopters blitzing the site hoping to snap a shot or two for *People* magazine. This wedding was a private, romantic, heartfelt event.

They exchanged their vows atop the Pacific clifftop, Patricia wearing a black vinyl suit and a leopard print jacket, clutching a wedding cake frosted in purple, Nic's favourite colour. She remembers 'stormy skies, crashing waves, dark woods – and everything out of focus except Nic in the centre with this light all around him'.

'He was real quiet,' commented Kathee McFarland of Nic at the wedding. 'Patty giggled a lot.' After the ten-minute ceremony, the pair posed for a couple of pictures, petted the attending sea otters then sped off to San Francisco in a blue Ferrari for lunch at the Cliffhouse restaurant.

'We love each other more than we ever have,' said Nic shortly afterwards. 'We've both been through enough to know that there are certain responsibilities and certain elements of work that have to go into a relationship. If the romance wears off, there needs to be stability and commitment – but I haven't felt any romance slipping away.'

Married life together meant big changes for both of them. Their two sons, Weston and Enzo, now stepbrothers, had to be catered for, although both boys had other parents in their lives. Patricia had asked Enzo what he thought of Nic. 'He's very honest. He would have said: "I don't like that guy." He didn't. I want to raise him and Weston with a liberal – and informed – attitude about everything.' Nic had to continue to honour the custody arrangement reached with Christina Fulton, and the two had remained close friends while raising Weston. Nic was also now on good friendly terms with Kristen Zang. 'She was happy for me and my wife,' he said of

Nic and his new wife, Patricia Arquette, at the premiere of her film Flirting With Disaster, *1996.*

her. However, the closeness of these ongoing friendships with Fulton and Zang would come to haunt Nic and Patricia within a year of getting married.

The first public appearance by the newly married couple was in May at the 1995 Cannes Film Festival in France. Nic was there to promote *Kiss Of Death*, while Patricia was doing promotional work for the release of *Beyond Rangoon*. With the marriage now made public, there was intense interest in the pair. Patricia also claimed the trip doubled as a honeymoon.

The celebrations were short-lived, as soon after Nic was awarded *People* magazine's not-at-all-coveted Worst Dressed award. 'He looks like a band leader off duty,' costume designer Bob Ringwood told *People* about a shiny green jacket he was photographed wearing in Las Vegas. 'Burn it,' advised *Another World*'s Dano. Designer Dennis Wingate said of him, 'He should dress really simply because he has such a distinctive face. He looks like he belongs in Vegas.' While RuPaul, transvestite model and singer not noted for understatement, commented: 'Nicolas Cage has his own personal style – and it's bad.'

Irritating features like that had the tendency to get under Cage's skin, necessitating an indulgence in the actor's favourite form of relaxation – a lengthy bath. 'Epsom salts, baking soda, sea salt, and David Bowie's *Low* – that's a good bath.' He'd also take out his frustrations on his gym equipment, having developed something of an addiction to working out for at least two hours each day. He employs a personal trainer, but has a tendency to lose his temper if spoken to while engaged in physical exercise. 'It becomes almost like a ritual in the day,' he said of his workout routine, which often took the form of a long, solitary run. 'You go through the pain and break walls down and get to clarity of some kind. That's what running is for me.'

There were other tensions he had to work his way through. While some family relationships improved others deteriorated during 1995 and into 1996. The good news was that his mother, Joy Vogelsang, had finally recovered from the mental illness and depression she had suffered during Nic's childhood and now lived not far from her famous son. She attended both the Golden Globe awards and the Oscars to support him. On the other hand, Nic's relationship with his father, August Coppola, had not improved. He had always been set against his son becoming an actor, and as Nic's career had progressed and he had followed his own intellectual pursuits around the world, father and son had communicated with each other mainly by fax or answering machine, rarely face-to-face. 'He left me a message that he had finished the book he was working on in Savannah,' Nic told the *San Francisco Chronicle*, while ruefully admitting that he had no idea what the book was about or why his father had gone to Savannah. 'I think he's in Paris now, with his wife,' he speculated.

Leaving Las Vegas caused a bizarre rift between father and son. August Coppola had publicly called the film his son's acting 'epitaph', presumably meaning that it would be a lasting achievement in his career. The press took a different view, reporting that August Coppola had claimed that *Leaving Las Vegas* would kill his son's career stone dead, that the film would be his 'epitaph'. 'It was misinterpreted,' Nic claimed. 'My father didn't mean I was ending my career. It was a big headline in *USA Today*, and that really bothered him. Now we're not talking. You know how it is – sometimes you're on the right wave and sometimes you're not.'

August was notably absent from the family group which attended the Oscar ceremony in 1996. As in the past, it was the Coppola side of the family who were causing Nic grief. He called the clan he couldn't escape 'passionate, competitive and crazy'.

Nic's first significant official recognition since the prize awarded to *Birdy* at Cannes almost ten years before came at the end of 1995. While Mike Figgis was touring the States promoting *Leaving Las Vegas* and getting secretly excited at the possibilities of Oscar nominations, he stopped off in Los Angeles to host an evening at the American Film Institute on Friday 20 October 1995 honouring the work of Nicolas Cage. In his diary for that day, Figgis noted: 'Back in L.A. and tonight there is the Nic Cage tribute which I'm hosting. Have no information and I think it will be "good luck with the improv." time. Don't even know where the cinema is or how I'm going to get there.'

Figgis needn't have worried. The evening proved to be a fine event. The tribute came at the AFI's ninth annual film festival held in Los Angeles. Nic was honoured along with another quirky actor, Christopher Walken, whose presentation was held the following day. 'Nicolas Cage and Christopher Walken are two of our most innovative, and creative actors,' AFI Director Jean Picker Firstenberg said. 'Constantly on the cutting edge, they have delivered consistently powerful performances in some of the most interesting films of the past decade. Nicolas Cage and Christopher Walken are truly deserving of this tribute, and AFI is proud to honour their work.' The previous year had seen two actors Nic Cage had worked with – Holly Hunter (*Raising Arizona*) and Dennis Hopper (*Red Rock West*) – honoured in this way. The same festival also presented a tribute to silent comic Buster Keaton – one of Cage's favourites and an inspiration for some of his work in *Moonstruck* and *Vampire's Kiss*.

The AFI described Cage's film portrayals as 'intense, often brooding and angst ridden', dubbing him 'one of today's most versatile young actors'. In a release to the media, the AFI noted: 'Cage first brought his alienated outsider persona to the screen in *Valley Girl*. Cage's portrayal of a tormented Vietnam vet in *Birdy* established him as a serious actor. Cage's roles in *Moonstruck, Raising Arizona* and *Wild At Heart* are the kind audiences talk about long after the movie is over.'

Featuring clips from many of his movies and the on-stage interview with Mike Figgis, the evening was a hit with the participants and audience alike. A week later, Figgis had noted his pleasant recollections of the evening in his diary: 'The evening with Nic went extremely well. There was no plan at all and we just winged it for two hours in front of a celebrity audience, including various Coppolas (Sofia is very stunning), Jim Carrey, Holly Hunter. I think we were pretty funny together.' The AFI tribute signalled the beginning of the Hollywood establishment's new attitude to Nicolas Cage – he was now to be taken seriously.

For *Leaving Las Vegas* Nicolas Cage had won a crateful of awards from critics' circles and film festivals across the United States. He was awarded the Best Actor accolade by the National Board of Review, the New York Film Critics' Circle, the Los Angeles Film Critics' Circle, the Boston Society of Film Critics, the Chicago Film Critics and the National Society of Film Critics; he was also given the same award by the San Sebastian Film Festival. He also received a Golden Globe Award for Best Actor in a Motion Picture (Drama) and the Screen Actors' Guild Award for Outstanding Performance by a Male Actor in Leading Role. 'I didn't go to college,' Nicolas Cage said in accepting the Screen Actors Guild award. 'This is my university, and I'm gonna consider this award my degree.' These were all wonderful accolades, but there was only one that really counted as a final seal of acceptance in Hollywood: the Best Actor Oscar.

'I'm being very Zen about it,' Nic said before nominations on the 13 February 1996. 'I'm not worried about Oscars. What I'm so encouraged about is the fact that my fellow actors are saying "good job". That's enough. I love acting. Acting is my therapy. Acting is my expression, my release.'

By the end of the day the nomination was in the bag and Nic's place at the 68th annual Academy Awards ceremony was booked. The other nominations were Anthony Hopkins (a previous winner for *Silence Of The Lambs*) for *Nixon*; Richard Dreyfus for *Mr Holland's Opus* (he'd also won before, in 1978 for *The Goodbye Girl*) and Italian actor Massimo Troisi for the Italian film *Il Postino*. Trois had died two days after completing the film, so his nomination was posthumous. Ironically, the fifth nominated actor was Cage's buddy Sean Penn, who'd been nominated for his role as the death-row prisoner in *Dead Man Walking* with Susan Sarandon.

The awards ceremony took place on the evening of 25 March 1996, by which time Nic had wrapped shooting on his next film, *The Rock*. This awards ceremony was Cage's chance to put himself alongside the other Coppolas who'd won Oscars: his grandfather, Carmine, had won (with Nino Rota) in 1974 for his score to *The Godfather, Part II*, in the same yeart as the Best Director Oscar went to Cage's Uncle, Francis Ford, for the same film.

Clad in a Hugo Boss tuxedo and with his wife along for the ride, Nic approached the Dorothy Chandler pavilion, the location of the ceremony, in the back of a slow-moving black limo. The pair had danced the tango in their Los Angeles apartment before leaving, in an attempt by Patricia to calm Nic's fraying nerves. Nic was tipped as a favourite to win, but the possibility of a sympathy vote for the late Massimo Troisi couldn't be discounted. And then, thought Nic, there was Sean Penn. His old pal had enjoyed a highly acclaimed career in a series of independent movies and this, just as for Nic, was his chance to reap the rewards. It was a long trip in that car, past crowds of film fans who lined the streets to watch the ritual procession of the stars to the Academy Awards.

'I had woken up in a good space and managed to go with it and relax,' Nic remembered later. 'Though people were using the term "front runner" I'm never one to assume anything. What would happen, I worried, if I got my hopes up and nothing happened because no one had seen the film? It gives you a kind of terrible stage fright when you start thinking. In some ways it was worse that I had been predicted to win. I didn't want to prepare a speech. I'd written one in case I won the Independent Spirit Award that was presented a few weeks earlier. When Sean Penn won that one, I crumpled up my speech and threw it out. It's not something you want to do to yourself and I was afraid that would happen again. When it comes down to the eleventh hour, you're going to get caught up in the excitement of the moment. You try to relax but then you start thinking about winning and you start thinking about losing. And you realise that winning is better than losing.'

The award for Best Actor would come at the end of the three-hour ceremony, which meant Nic and Patricia had to sit through award after award and watch a host of daft musical numbers intended to reflect the range of films selected for the Oscars that year. When the time came, Nic was more tired than excited. 'Then Jessica Lange opened the envelope,' he remembered. 'I could hear her utter the letter "N". She hadn't even got the rest of my first name out and I knew I was in. I took it all in. I even remembered to breathe. It was a damn fine moment. It's not something that happens every day.'

Nic made his way to the podium to accept his award, desperately trying to think of what to say in lieu of the speech he'd neglected to draft. 'Oh, boy!' he said, up there in front of the movers and shakers of Hollywood, the superstars and decision makers, not to mention millions of TV viewers around the globe. 'A $3.5 million budget, some 16-millimetre stock footage thrown in, and I'm holding one of these!' Nic held the figure of the little golden man coveted by most of the actors and actresses in the audience in front of him.

It had been a long haul and a diverse bunch of parts that had brought him to this place at this time. 'It told me I wasn't crazy all these years,' said Cage of the award. 'The fact that the Academy noticed me was really brave of them, and good for the industry and the future of alternative movies. The award encouraged me to keep following my heart. There had been a reason for what I did and the Oscar said that my ideas weren't wrong. When you get an Oscar, you are being recognised by your peers and that was important to me. The prejudice I experienced because of my name was like a pitchfork in my butt and it made me work twice as hard at everything I did. The Oscar took fifteen years, but it took care of all the past hurts.'

September 1996 saw yet another accolade being paid to the maverick actor – a Lifetime Achievement Award at the Montreal World Film Festival.

Ushered by an appreciative (mostly French-Canadian) audience into Montreal's Thé âtre Jean-Duceppe, Cage was interviewed by Darrah Meely, a well-known film critic, cinephile, educator and producer, who compressed his fifteen-year career in cinema into a couple of hours. Wearing a sober dark suit and tie, Cage looked the part of an acting veteran basking in the glory of recognition and accolades. It was a part he hadn't played much before. At 33, Nic was the youngest ever actor to be given Montreal's Lifetime Achievement Award.

Nic and Patricia at the Golden Globe awards, 1996. Nic received the award for Best Actor in a Motion Picture (Drama).

He spoke in the interview of trying to find a niche for himself, a way of making the kind of oddball movies he was interested in. He highlighted his desire to 'go further than naturalism' in his acting style, to 'stay true to your instincts' and 'fight for things before they get snuffed out' by the Hollywood machine. Nic revealed how he liked to see dailies (the raw, unedited footage shot the previous day and screened each morning of shooting for the director) and take a pro-active part in developing his characters, such as studying the storyboards of *Raising Arizona* to capture the cartoonish nature of the part.

Nic discussed his method-acting roots, revealing how as he matured he'd moved away from the obviousness of some method approaches. 'I didn't really have any proper training,' he said of his beginnings. 'I thought everything had to be real. On the set of *Racing With The Moon*, I cut myself because I thought I'd really feel the pain. I was crazy. On *Vampire's Kiss*, I ate the cockroach because the script called for it. Today, fifteen years later, maybe I'm not so obsessive about acting. I have a wife and child to be with now.'

However, having the wife and child didn't stop rumours circulating now he was big news. Just around the time of their first anniversary, Patricia and Nic were upset by a story sweeping Hollywood that the pair were about to divorce. She was accused of having an affair with Ben Stiller, the director-star of *Flirting With Disaster* which she'd made on location in Arizona in 1996. Nic was said to have taken up with his ex-girlfriend Kristen Zang, despite the fact that she'd been linked with actor Leonardo DiCaprio for some time. Nic's close relationship with Christina Fulton was also studied, following the revelation that he often spent evenings and entire nights at Christina's flat.

It was hard for the pair to counter the stories, though they both made a strong stab at it. 'People are always looking at you when you're out,' Patricia said, repeating the complaints echoed by many celebrity couples who hadn't withstood the pressure of public interest, including Johnny Depp and Winona Ryder, Depp and Kate Moss, and Brad Pitt and Gwyneth Paltrow. 'We don't go out a lot, but if we do and we're in a crabby mood, people look at us and go: "Ooh, are there problems?" Friends call in the middle of the night because they've just heard we're getting divorced. I pass the phone to Nicolas so they can hear we're still together.'

The worry about the tales being told was enough for Nic to pass on accepting another role offered to him by his *Leaving Las Vegas* director Mike Figgis. Despite their successful Oscar-winning collaboration, he opted out of *One Night Stand*, which the director started shooting in May 1996 from a Joe Eszterhas script. Nic said he felt he didn't quite fit the role, but the real reason seems to have been the prospect of playing an adulterous character when his own marriage was just approaching its first anniversary. The role was eventually taken by Wesley Snipes, who starred opposite Natasja Kinski. Nic had done well to avoid the project, as Figgis had a battle on his hands when scriptwriter Joe Eszterhas took his name off the production due to extensive rewrites by the director.

Nic was equally angry about the insinuations people were making about the state of the relationship between him and Patricia and the inferences drawn from his friendships with Kristen and Christina. 'All I can say about that is that some people take a good thing and turn it into a bad thing,' he said in reaction to tabloid reports that he'd renewed his relationship with Christina Fulton and had moved back in with her. 'Sometimes I'm working late and Weston has to go to bed, so it's easier for me to just go over there and have dinner and say: "Hi, how was your day?" than to keep him up all night and bring him over to my house.'

Nic had no problems with the fact that his wife was also on good terms with Paul Rossi, the father of Enzo. 'Patricia and I understand there are other people in each of our children's lives,' he said, admitting they had considered the possibility of one day having a child together, 'but not right now because we're both very busy. We have our hands full.'

Nic and Patricia claimed their marriage, far from falling apart, was stronger than ever as it entered its second year. 'We're really happy,' he claimed. 'We support each other. We're a sounding board for each other's frustrations. She'll suggest ideas to me or I'll suggest ideas to her for how to play a character. It's wonderful.'

For the moment Nic was where he'd wanted to be as an actor. He'd gone his own route, often to the derision of others, but he had emerged triumphant. He had even had the old Zenith TV from the sixties that had inspired his acting ambitions repaired. This came about after he talked about the broken television now stored in the loft on TV chat shows following the Oscar win, repeating that it was the flickering, magical, black-and-white world that he saw which first got him interested in acting. Shortly afterwards he was contacted by a representative of Zenith. 'They want to fix my TV for me,' declared a delighted Nic, 'which is great!'

10. New Age Action Man

I N AN ASTONISHING CHANGE OF direction, Nic followed up his art-house hit by promptly reinventing himself as a most unlikely action hero. Nic had changed direction before, from his offbeat oddball roles to a series of hit-and-miss comedies, but no-one expected Hollywood's one-time king of goofy characters to take on the likes of Arnold Schwarzenegger, Sylvester Stallone or Bruce Willis in the action movie stakes.

'I have to admit that I really enjoy action movies,' he claimed when he began work on *The Rock* – even before he'd won the Oscar for *Leaving Las Vegas*. 'It's a style I have not mastered yet.' The nearest he had come previously to playing an action role had been in the flop *Fire Birds* (*Wings Of The Apache*) in 1990.

Taking the starring role in *The Rock* was not to be a one-off indulgence. It was part of a project he was developing, a desire to play a less muscle-bound, more reluctant or vulnerable type of big-screen action hero. To that end he made three overblown action epics in a row – *The Rock, Con Air* and *Face/Off*. 'For some reasons, genre movies tend to come in threes for me,' he noted, to which his *Leaving Las Vegas* director Mike Figgis retorted: 'They come in threes if you let them.'

Nic had signed on to star in *The Rock* before he won the Oscar for *Leaving Las Vegas*, but the acclaim that film had drawn served to up his fee considerably. Whereas he'd come down from his going rate of around $4 million per film to $240,000 for Mike Figgis's movie, *The Rock* offered the $4 million, *Con Air* paid him $6 million, while *Face/Off* also offered $6 million, plus an additional $250,000 if he won the Oscar, and another $250,000 if *The Rock* grossed more than $100 million. Nicolas Cage had hit the financial big time.

'The genre is lacking in character,' he said of action movies, identifying what he felt he could bring to the top grossing film genre of the nineties. 'Many of the action heroes are robotic supermen you can't really feel for, with the exception of maybe Harrison Ford, Sean Connery and Clint Eastwood. The invincible male figure is limited, and I hope to find a different approach; reluctant heroes, flawed convicts, action movies where the emphasis is placed on acting.'

He may have had high hopes, but his work in his action movie trio showed that he could indeed bring something unique to the genre. In his early thirties he was also significantly younger than the other movie action men, who by the late nineties were all in their fifties, with the notable exception of Sean Connery, Nic's co-star in *The Rock* – who was 65. Their energy for running from speeding cars, dodging bullets and leaping from explosions was limited. Hollywood was ready for a new kind of hero, a new icon for a new type of action movie.

The Rock came from the stable of producers Don Simpson and Jerry Bruckheimer, who since the mid-eighties had enjoyed phenomenal success in the action movie genre, producing films like *Beverly Hills Cop, Top Gun, Days Of Thunder, Bad Boys* (launching the movie career of Will Smith) and the submarine drama *Crimson Tide*. Overblown action-adventure films were their trademark, and as they entered the second half of the nineties, there was nowhere left for the genre to go but to ever more ludicrous extremes, hence the indulgent excesses of *The Rock* and *Con Air*.

In *The Rock* Nic was cast as the wonderfully named Stanley Goodspeed, an FBI chemical weapons expert who is teamed up with John Mason (Sean Connery), a British Secret Service agent who is the only man ever to have broken out of Alcatraz, the prison island in San Francisco Bay. Their task now is to break into the prison, to take on rogue general Francis Hummel (Ed Harris) and his men who are trying to blackmail the American government by threatening to fire four missiles with chemical warheads at San Francisco. It's an all-action, over-the-top extravaganza, with comical character moments featuring Nic and Connery which mark the film out as something beyond normal action fare.

'We all knew there was no character on the page at the beginning,' Nic said of the cipher he encountered when he read the original screenplay for *The Rock*. 'I saw Stanley as a different kind of action hero, a reluctant one who is not heroic because he's got a steroid-ripped body or a robot head. I wanted to play a decent man who doesn't have an interest in killing and who doesn't swear.'

Production of *The Rock* proved to be chaotic, allowing Nic much more leeway than he otherwise might have had. Director Michael Bay had co-ordinated the automobile mayhem of *Bad Boys*, but he'd never faced anything on the scale of *The Rock*. Jerry Bruckheimer was taking the largest hand in the production, as his partner Don Simpson was too busy pursuing the hedonistic drugs 'n' sex lifestyle that was to lead to his death in January 1996. A variety of writers had taken a crack at the script, including – bizarrely enough – British sitcom writing duo Dick Clement and Ian La Frenais (better known for seventies comedy shows *The Likely Lads* and *Porridge* than for action blockbusters). The final screenplay was credited to David Weisberg and Douglas Cook, but Bruckheimer had a big hand in the constant rewrites which took place during production.

This all suited Nic who just went his own way, inventing character stuff which found its way into the movie. He began by changing his character's name from Bill to Stanley, feeling it was more 'right' for the role. He also concocted incidental character details, like a devotion to the Beatles. 'Early on I went into the office and I

Sean Connery was very impressed by Nic's approach to acting in The Rock*: 'I found him totally professional. That really is something in this day and age.'*

said, "Look this guy has no dignity, this Stan Goodspeed character. He's an FBI agent who hates his job and wants to get in the field and wants to start shooting things up with a gun. We can't have that, 'cause I can't play that with dignity." I think people who like their jobs are cool, so let's make him really like his job, make him really smart. He's just trying to stay alive. It gave me a chance to open up the doors a little bit and play the fear and the irreverence that the character feels towards the John Mason character.'

There was more to Nic's involvement in the film than just turning up and playing the part. It was the beginning of a serious interest in what took place behind the scenes of a film. 'The fact of the matter is I rewrote most of my dialogue,' he claimed. 'It just wasn't on the page. There were a lot of cooks in the kitchen. Jerry Bruckheimer is very similar to my Uncle Francis in that way. Things are always being changed, being tweaked.'

The writers – David Weisberg and Douglas Cook – took exception to everyone involved claiming the credit for *The Rock*. 'Nic Cage, Sean Connery, Michael Bay and Jerry Bruckheimer would not have been there if it had not been for our writing the dialogue and creating the characters. For Nic Cage to look at a line he rewrote and take responsibility is insulting. It remains ours – the characters, the story, the action are the same as we wrote,' claimed Weisberg.

Whatever the on-set tensions, all movies are collaborative products, and Nic had more input than most actors into those elements of *The Rock* that made the film a success. Above all, the role was fun for Nic, who felt he had returned to his back yard, playing at movie making with his brother Christopher. 'It was probably the most expensive movie I have ever made, but for some reason I got that Super-8 feeling I had when I was a kid and my brother and I used to make movies. It was like, "OK, now you're gonna fall down – then you pick up the gun." Ironically, the bigger the movie and the more action, the more it feels like playing in the back yard.'

There were drawbacks to filming on location on Alcatraz, which is now a tourist attraction. 'The interior of the place is sinister and the weather is quick to change,' said Nic, who dubbed the location 'Tetanus World'. 'I felt silly complaining about it, because I'm just an actor.'

Working with Sean Connery was a big thrill – Nic had followed all the James Bond movies and had identified with Connery when he'd been a kid going to the movies with his father. 'I remember asking him all kinds of questions,' Nic said of his time with Connery. 'I saw it as an opportunity to really examine all the thoughts and concerns I had about acting. I always emulated his career in some ways. I hope to be lucky enough to enjoy some semblance of what he's been able to achieve. He's probably the only superstar I know that can do action movies and then do an in-depth character in a dramatic movie and go back and forth.'

Working together, Nic and Connery approached the sometimes daft dialogue they had as a form of music, finding rhythms for each line and delivering them as if they were parts of a larger symphony. 'We both hear the rhythm and the music of the lines and we play them just like we're playing an instrument. That made it easy to work with him. Well, you can hear that in his movies, can't you?' Nic claimed of Connery's past movie characters. 'Think about some of his roles – that voice, almost singing the lines. Once we found out how we shared this feeling, everything else just fell into place.'

Connery confirmed their unusual approach to action-movie making: 'Every line has its own natural rhythm. The trick is – the effort is – to find it. Nic is very good at that. He has a great ear, and that makes him a good partner in acting.' In fact, Sean Connery, well known as a tough taskmaster and not one to suffer fools gladly, seems to have been impressed by Nic's approach to acting: 'I found him totally professional. That is really something in this day and age.'

Like Connery, Nic was keen to leave difficult aspects of the production up to the professionals – particularly the stunt men. 'I'm not a macho actor and I don't do my own stunts,' he admitted, his personal feelings feeding into the reluctant action hero he was playing. 'I don't understand actors that make such a big deal out of doing their own stunts, saying "Wow, I'm a tough man, I did it myself." I'm a dad. I want to be around to see my kid grow up. The other guy [the stuntman] needs a job to do, he needs to make some money.'

The Rock proved to be an eye-opener for Nic. 'I will tell you the truth, this is the hardest I've ever had to work on a movie,' he admitted.

The cast and crew working on *The Rock* were shocked when news reached them of the drug-related death of Bruckheimer's production partner Don Simpson. Bruckheimer attempted to keep the news under wraps until the end of filming on that particular Friday in January 1996, but Nic found out. 'Somebody accidentally told me. It's difficult to concentrate when one of the conductors dies and you're still doing the piece.' Director Michael Bay picked up on Nic's sombre mood, and asked what was wrong. The actor had no option but to tell him the news. Filming finished immediately, while the production regrouped.

The Rock boasted a $25 million opening weekend from 9 June 1996, with an eventual $134 million gross in the United States and an astonishing $335 million worldwide. It was the blockbuster movie of the summer of 1996, rivalling Tom Cruise's *Mission: Impossible* for box office supremacy. It was Nicolas Cage's own biggest commercial hit by far, eclipsing his previous best, the $80 million gross of *Moonstruck.* The movie also set a video rental record for the United States as the most ordered film, with 830,000 copies purchased by the big retailers in advance of the release. Nicolas Cage had arrived as Hollywood's new vulnerable action icon.

Chicago Sun-Times film critic Roger Ebert dubbed *The Rock* 'a first-rate, slam-bang action thriller with a lot of style and no little humor . . . What really works is the chemistry between Connery and Cage . . . There are several Identikit Hollywood action stars who can occupy the centre of chaos like this, but not many can make it look like they think they're really there.' *USA Today* claimed that 'Cage

Nic gives the all-clear at the end of The Rock.

is funny . . . the movie, at least, knows it is junk and has fun playing off that fact without posing as something more.'

For *Entertainment Weekly*, *The Rock* was 'a machine designed to pummel audiences into submission . . . Cage and Connery inject tasty bits of personality into their roles. Cage, happily, doesn't have to abandon the charismatic zigzags in mood – the leaps from goofiness to rage – that have marked his performances in movies like *Leaving Las Vegas*. He plays right to the gallery with his gleam of soulful scepticism and his funky, off-kilter line readings, as when he says to Connery, "How, in the name of Zeus' butthole, did you get out of your cell?"' That was a line that Nic had concocted himself and fought to get into the movie.

Even before he'd won the Oscar for *Leaving Las Vegas*, Nic had agreed to star in the action movie double whammy which would dominate the box office in the summer of 1997: *Con Air* and *Face/Off.*

If *The Rock* served as his entree in the action movie stakes, *Con Air* was to be the main course. The film was a huge production, ending up on screen as some out-of-control comic-book epic with a ridiculous life of its own. Even more than *The Rock*, *Con Air* displayed a healthy self-awareness, a kind of parody of the action movie genre without being silly for the sake of it. The audience were quickly clued in to the fact that the actors and producers knew the film was over-the-top, but wasn't the ride fun?

Bruckheimer, with whom Nic had forged a bond on *The Rock*, was also the producer of *Con Air*. He bought the speculative script from Scott Rosenberg, who had enjoyed some success writing *Things To Do In Denver When You're Dead*, a thriller starring Andy Garcia. Rosenberg had become aware of the existence of a US Marshal's prisoner air transport service from a newspaper article, and had written his screenplay after a fact-finding visit to the outfit's Oklahoma City base. 'I spent three days on the Con Air plane with the convicts,' recalled Rosenberg of his research period. 'We flew all over the country. These guys were in a really bad mood.'

Bruckheimer snapped up the script, but felt it needed further development. 'It was certainly great writing,' he noted, 'but I instantly surmised that it needed more heart. It had to be character-driven, which is a common theme throughout all of my films, no matter what the action content might be.' Bruckheimer signed up director Simon West to handle the film, even though the British commercials director had never made any kind of feature length film, never mind a blockbuster action flick. He was best known for shooting the video for Mel and Kim's 'Respectable'.

Nic had already expressed 'some interest' in starring in Bruckheimer's next epic, so a meeting was convened between him, Bruckheimer and Simon West to discuss *Con Air* and whether the leading role of ex-convict Cameron Poe would suit Cage. The meeting took place the very evening that Nic won the Screen Actors' Guild Award, and the odds were rising that the Best Actor Oscar would be his. Bruckheimer couldn't envisage anyone else in the role. 'Nicolas is the consummate pro,' he said, echoing the praise of Sean Connery. 'He brings everything of himself to each role he

Nicolas Cage was instrumental in developing the character of Cameron Poe, hero of Con Air.

plays. He always invests a great deal of time into his character and into the script.'

West and Nic discussed Cameron Poe, his background and how he fitted into the action of the film. Poe was an Army Ranger convicted of accidentally killing a thug who'd been harassing his pregnant wife. Sent to jail, he waited for the day he could be released to meet the daughter he'd never seen. When finally let out, he hitched a ride with the government's prisoner air transport service, hoping to get home for his daughter's birthday. However, some of the baddest cons in the US penal system were also on the plane, which they planned to hijack in a bid for freedom. Only Poe could stop them.

These initial discussions allowed Nic even more input into his character and the film generally than he'd had on *The Rock*. The prologue and scenes featured under the opening credits which show Poe serving his jail time and writing to his daughter were his idea, drawn from his feeling for his own son, Weston. 'Nic is always contributing ideas to the film,' Bruckheimer confirmed. 'It was his concept to make Poe a decorated Army Ranger, which adds tremendously to the power of the character and the empathy you feel for him. I love working with Nicolas because he is totally and deeply involved in every aspect of the film and his role. He's an incredible talent and one of the finest actors in our business.'

Nic was grateful that in Bruckheimer he'd found a producer who would allow him to develop his vulnerable action hero persona. 'He genuinely cares about the balance between action and character development,' the actor said of the producer. 'Ironically, working on action movies – with this great guiding force of a producer –

Con Air *saw Nic Cage make a spectacular return to Las Vegas – by crashing a plane into the famous Sands Hotel.*

allows me to do more writing, to be more involved in the creative process. *Con Air* has been a very fulfilling experience.'

Director Simon West was a big fan of Nic's work and was pleased when the actor came on board. 'Nicolas Cage is one of the greatest actors around today. I've always been a big fan. You never see the same character twice from him in any performance,' said West, who also had good, solid commercial reasons for casting Nic in the lead role. 'Once I had Nic Cage on board, it was much easier to cast the rest of the parts, because people really wanted to work with him. At the time he'd just won his Oscar for *Leaving Las Vegas*. There were so many good roles in this movie, it reminded me of one of those classic war films, like *The Great Escape* or *The Dirty Dozen*. I tried to get the best actor I could find for each part.'

West ended up with a starry cast. John Cusack signed on as US Marshal Vince Larkin, the man on the ground who helps Cage defeat the gang; *Star Trek* actor Colm Meany puts in a brilliantly comic turn as abusive Drug Enforcement Agency man Malloy; while the criminal gang featured John Malkovich, suitably over-the-top as Cyrus 'the Virus' Grissom, Steve Buscemi as serial killer Garland Greene and Ving Rhames (from *Pulp Fiction* and *ER*) as Diamond Dog. When Nic thought the Federal guard on the plane should be a woman, actress Rachel Ticotin was cast in what had been envisaged as a male role.

West was pleased with what Nic brought to his role as the obsessed ex-con trying to keep his nose clean, desperate to get home to see his eight-year-old daughter and bring her a present of a stuffed bunny rabbit – the source of much of the film's comic relief and over-the-top lines, many of them developed by Nic himself. It was he who came up with a running joke about his protecting the stuffed rabbit, culminating in the line: 'Put the bunny back in the box.' 'Yeah, I was trying to find a symbolic metaphor for the love Cameron has for his child in the middle of all this hell, and also a way to extract humor,' Nic admitted. 'By writing that scene, I wanted to have a straightforward, tough-guy attitude about the bunny rabbit.'

'In this, he's completely different from anything else he's done before,' claimed Simon West of his star. 'I've never seen anyone so inventive and experimental. He's amazing to watch. The work he puts into a role is very impressive.' Nic's dedication was such that he went to Alabama to work on his accent for the movie, all the while thinking up new ways of improving the script or adding little bits of character business here and there. It was his way of keeping himself interested.

'Nic Cage was very precise,' West noted. 'He would be up the night before, rewriting lines and having a very strong take on how he was going to do each particular scene. He would come on and his first take would be brilliant and great, but then he would talk about what we were going to do for another five minutes, and go back and do a second take, and it would be just as good if not better. Then he would do a third take – just, you know, for an alternative, but really any one of them was fine.'

As a neophyte director, West found that Nic was driving the action rather than him. 'I've gotten to the point that I direct myself quite a bit,' Nic claimed, although he denied having any real directorial ambitions. 'I don't think I have the energy or discipline to be a director. It's just too much work for me, just everybody, all the time, needing you. I've been pretty lucky with directors. It's so important to work with people who care, where it's not about money.'

Nic wasn't too worried about appearances, either. Over the years his hair had become ever thinner on top of his head. For Cameron Poe he had shoulder-length attachments woven into it. He refuses to wear wigs in movies to cover up his ever-increasing baldness, preferring to avoid the ludicrous hair pieces which his *The Rock* co-star Sean Connery once insisted on. 'It's part of an actor's ability to create, like when Lon Chaney used different prostheses,' he said, arguing that he would only ever wear a hairpiece if a role demanded it – otherwise, what you see is what you get. 'In *Leaving Las Vegas*, there I am with all my hairline glory in front of God and everybody. I'm fine with it. I don't really think it's an issue.'

Nic's research for *Con Air* was meticulous. Along with Bruckheimer, West and screenwriter Scott Rosenberg, he visited Fulsom maximum security prison to soak up the atmosphere. Just days before the trip he had won the Oscar and was greeted with a welcoming roar by the inmates, some of America's most irredeemable criminals. 'He was really touched that they even knew who he was,' according to Bruckheimer.

Nic also put a lot of effort into working up some muscles, something he hadn't done since *Kiss Of Death*. He spent several hours each day for weeks prior to and during the production working out and lifting weights with his trainer Lee Nichol and kick boxing champion Benny Urquidez. Nichol also put him on a strict diet, to help him tone and

During production on Con Air, *co-producers Disney complained that Nic Cage had 'too many muscles' even for an action hero.*

bulk up his muscle, reducing his body fat to a mere 3 per cent of his total body weight. 'It was weird. At one point Disney was worried I was getting too big and I was looking kind of scary,' he said of the concerns of the film's co-producers. 'I thought, "Well, that's a new one – too many muscles for an action movie!"' During filming he came up with numerous reasons for Poe to take his shirt off to show off his new physique.

West also found himself dealing with some remaining method-acting ticks. He claimed that every couple of days, in between takes, Nic would begin shrieking and howling. He'd take a running leap at a wall, where he would cling on, screaming until he was told to come down. Nic claimed he was keeping his energy up and relieving frustrations, but West believed his star actor was pretending to be Spiderman. On other occasions, Nic would slip into charm mode. 'Nic's very, very charming,' claimed West. 'One day one of the girls on the camera crew sneezed, and he said – in character, in his southern drawl – "A man could fall in love with you just for the way you sneeze." She just melted, and all the women on the set went weak at the knees.'

Principal photography on *Con Air* began in Salt Lake City with work on its many airport scenes, before the cast and crew relocated to Ogden in Utah to shoot an exchange of prisoners at the local airstrip. A month was spent shooting in the tiny town of Wendover on the Utah/Nevada border where all the action surrounding the grounded plane was filmed. The climatic finale of the film saw Nic return to Las Vegas.

'One draft of the script had the plane crashing into the White House,' noted Jerry Bruckheimer. 'I didn't quite believe that. We also decided against having the plane clip the arm of the Statue of Liberty. I said the guys would really rather crash into Las Vegas. So we took our convicts and brought the plane down to land on Las Vegas Boulevard, about 50 yards from the Sands Hotel.' West had read in the *Los Angeles Times* that this famous hotel was due for demolition and saw a unique opportunity. He and Bruckheimer managed to persuade the developers to delay the demolition so that they could crash their plane into the hotel for real. It was to be the special effects climax of the film.

Using a fifteen ton C-123 plane which had the interior gutted to make it lighter, the special effects crew and Simon West prepared to make movie history. 'There's no complicated blocking of actors,' said West. 'You've just got a plane running over a casino, and that's it.' The effects shot cost a total of half a million dollars to pull off. Safety was an important issue as the film had already suffered one casualty, when Phillip Swartz, a 39-year-old with a wife and four daughters, who worked for special effects contractor Special Effects Unlimited on the Utah exterior shoot, had been crushed to death when one of the plane mock-ups collapsed on top of him.

The effects team estimated that, launched from a six-foot-tall ramp, the plane could reach speeds of up to 50 miles an hour as it covered the hundred-yard stretch from the launch point to the hotel foyer. Just before starting the shot assistant effects co-ordinator Paul Lombardi attempted to clear the scene: 'Stunt guys, be aware – this thing is coming in angry. It will eat you.' Two takes were necessary over two nights to capture the action when the first attempt failed after a tow-line snapped. A little post-

Nic is happy to leave stunts to the stuntmen. 'I'm a dad. I want to be around to see my kids grow up.'

139

production special effects trickery completed the breathtaking finale to the film.

Con Air opened almost a year to the day after *The Rock*, pulling in $24 million over the opening weekend from 8 June 1997. By early September, it had easily flown over the $100 million mark in United States grosses alone. *The Rock* had been no fluke, even though Bruckheimer had been worried about producing *Con Air* without a star like Sean Connery to prop up Nic. 'We don't know if he can open a picture by himself in foreign markets, because *The Rock* had Sean Connery. So this will tell the story,' Bruckheimer said, candidly.

'Do I feel the pressure? Sure,' Nic admitted, before the film opened. 'Because, you know, people spent a lot of money on *Con Air* [reportedly more than $70 million]. There's a sense that I need to really make this movie perform well. But at the end of the day, I'm an actor and what I'm mostly responsible for is whether or not my acting comes through.'

It was the reviewers who had to decide whether Nic's performance shone through all the pyrotechnics and over-the-top antics. *USA Today* dubbed the film the 'fast, funny and robustly acted progeny of *The Rock*,' while *Entertainment Weekly* felt that 'Nicolas Cage gets right into the you-won't-believe-this-but-then-neither-do-we spirit of it all. He sports long hippie locks that give him a saintly, Christ-gone-Rambo look, and he speaks in a noble over-deliberate drawl that makes him even more of a walking put-on than he was as the Elvis-in-snakeskin hipster of *Wild At Heart.*' However, the *Chicago Sun-Times* critic Roger Ebert didn't approve of Nic's turn as Cameron Poe. 'Cage makes the wrong choice, I think, by playing Cameron Poe as a slow-witted Elvis type who is very, very earnest and approaches every task with tunnel vision.' It was the first time in many years that Ebert, normally a Cage admirer, had given the star a bad review.

Nicolas Cage wasn't finished with the action movie genre just yet and served up *Face/Off* for dessert. This time out he got to play a bad guy, the villain of the piece – an excellent chance for some demented overacting, but also something of a risk after his nice-guy heroes and comedy fall guys. 'I felt like this character was someone who would have a Chihuahua stuck in his basal ganglia [parts of the brain],' Nic explained bizarrely of how he turned the relatively straightforward bad-guy role of Castor Troy (another great character name to follow Stanley Goodspeed and Cameron Poe) into an out-and-out cartoon lunatic. 'He's a song-and-dance kind of bad guy. So when John Travolta [playing the good guy on Cage's trail] was holding a gun to my head, and I was saying "I think you better pull the trigger because I'm ready" – then all of a sudden I started singing, to freak John Travolta's character out. So I started singing like a bad seventies rock star – "I'm ready, ready for the big ride, baby!"'

Face/Off was a bizarre project from the beginning which went on to enjoy great success upon its summer release in 1997. Its Director, John Woo, had arrived in America after an acclaimed action-movie career in Hong Kong where he'd made a star of actor Chow Yun Fat. He started in the States making brainless Jean Claude Van Damme action movies, with *Hard Target* in 1993, before hitting the big time with

Nic in Face/Off, *John Woo's high-octane identity switch thriller.*

Broken Arrow, a 1996 nuclear hijack thriller featuring John Travolta and Christian Slater. *Face/Off* turned out to be the ideal combination of Woo's Hong Kong action trademarks and a Hollywood sci-fi plot.

Shooting for *Face/Off* started early in 1997, immediately after Nic had wrapped on *Con Air*, but the film had its genesis some seven years earlier. Writers Mike Werb and Michael Colleary, who wrote the first draft of their screenplay in 1990, described the film as 'a psychological thriller disguised as an action film'. Neither writer had ever seen a John Woo movie at the time, claiming their inspiration came from films like Raoul Walsh's crime thriller *White Heat*, starring James Cagney, and John Frankenheimer's identity switch thriller *Seconds*, starring Rock Hudson.

In fact, the film had started life as a sci-fi extravaganza set 100 years into the future. Director John Woo turned the project down in this form around 1992, leaving actor-producer Michael Douglas to try and revive it. At one stage Douglas was intending to co-star in the film with Harrison Ford. Woo found himself drawn back to *Face/Off*, which by then was languishing in development hell under the nonsense title of *Switcheroo*. 'I suggested the studio take out 95 per cent of the sci-fi stuff and make the movie more of a character-based story,' Woo recalled.

'When I saw Woo's *The Killer* for the first time I was staggered,' admitted Colleary. 'The way people moved in the film was like watching live animation. It was the most cinematic thing I had ever seen: brilliantly and kinetically directed. Without knowing John Woo or being familiar with his work at the time, I realised that we had written a John Woo movie.' Having Woo direct their script was, according to Colleary, 'the culmination of all my hopes and ambitions'.

Following their teaming on *Broken Arrow*, John Travolta and John Woo were quickly together for *Face/Off*, but they needed an actor to play the bad guy opposite Travolta. 'John Woo and I were in from the start,' said Travolta, 'and we went to Nic. We really wanted him to join in. I'm so happy he did. Nic and I have, shall we say, an attraction for the bizarre, the outlandish, so putting us together was kind of dangerous.'

In the plot-twisting high-tech thriller relentless FBI agent Sean Archer (Travolta) must go dangerously undercover to investigate the location of a lethal biological weapon planted by his arch rival, the sadistic terrorist-for-hire Castor Troy (Cage), who was responsible for the death of Archer's son six years before. By means of radical surgery, Archer literally 'borrows' Troy's face and identity so as to convince his paranoid convict brother Pollux that he is Castor and thus discover the location of the bomb. Things take a twist when Troy, emerging from coma after the switch, takes the only available face and transforms into Archer. He wreaks havoc upon Archer's life, both at work and at home. As the bomb continues to count down, the tension mounts. Surprisingly, the bomb plot is taken care of halfway through, with the rest of the film being a high-stakes game of cat-and-mouse as Archer and Troy, ironically trapped within each other's identities, try to save their own faces.

With the potential to confuse the audience, not to mention the actors who end up playing each other, Woo had his work cut out keeping track of *Face/Off*. The result was a surprisingly clear and easy to follow summer blockbuster which was to gain Travolta, Woo and Nic some of the best reviews of their careers.

'They are the yin and the yang,' Nic said of the characters he and Travolta played. 'Archer has lost his grip and passion for life. Castor, on the other hand, has a huge appetite for life, more specifically for sex, money, gold and killing.' Instead of playing twins, as actors generally do to play both good and evil within the same movie, Travolta and Nic not only had to switch places from good guy to bad guy, but they also had to mirror each other's performances to pull off the astonishing conceit at the film's centre.

It was a challenge for song-and-dance man John Travolta – whose career had been brought back from the dead by Quentin Tarantino's *Pulp Fiction* – to capture the nuances of Nic's typically out-of-his-head turn as Castor Troy. 'It's always fun when an evil part is well written,' said Travolta of the switch he makes. 'Nic is so specific – he has this vocal cadence, an almost poetic elongated speech. His walk is very distinctive. I felt that the combination really allowed me to have fun with it, more than it being difficult. It was challenging, because I had to be very thorough with it.'

Nic agreed and noted how Travolta 'borrowed' some of his own trademark mannerisms. 'He was copying the walk from the first time we met on the movie. I noticed quite a bit of copying in terms of the cadence of the way I speak, slowing things down a little bit, with a sort of grandiose flair to certain deliveries.'

'It's a bold and unique way of telling a story,' affirmed executive producer Steven

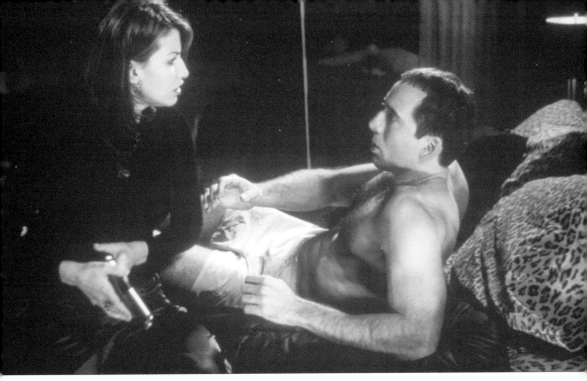

Same face, different man. Nic's girlfriend (Gina Gershon) doesn't know that she is really talking to FBI agent Sean Archer.

Reuther. 'There's a symmetry to the characters despite their violent confrontation.' Producer Terence Chang, with whom Woo has worked for the previous eighteen years, added that '*Face/Off* is the perfect vehicle for John because it's about two guys who are inherently good and evil. It's not just an action film but a powerful, emotional story with values. There is never just action for action's sake in a John Woo movie.'

'It may be the first time two actors have ever had to jointly choose what a character does,' John Travolta explained. Cage agreed that their approach to the roles was groundbreaking and original. 'Switching identities in the script gave John and me a chance to capture the essence and cadences of one another and run with the characters. It really was a kind of collective acting experience.'

Executive producer Jonathan D. Krane knew the process would be difficult. 'We realised early on that making this movie was going to be an incredible process because each character had to have his own idiosyncrasies, and when the actor becomes the other character those idiosyncrasies have to be imitated.' Chang thought the production had signed up the perfect cast. 'Travolta and Cage are perfect because they're both so charismatic and equally believable as a good guy and a bad guy and mimic each other with perfect precision, always surprising the audience.'

Actress Joan Allen, who had played a high-school girl in *Peggy Sue Got Married*, found herself in an action movie for the first time, playing Travolta's grief-stricken wife, Dr Eve Archer. She was fascinated by the transformation of the two actors into each other. 'To see John and Nic move between Sean Archer and Castor Troy is an incredible thing. To watch their ability to copy body positions, gestures, vocal rhythms and patterns is amazing.'

'Make it bigger, do it quicker and make it better,' was the credo of producer Barrie Osborne for *Face/Off*, knowing that the film had to follow the successes of *The Rock* and *Con Air*. With a spectacular high-speed boat chase, plane crash, careening humvees and helicopter acrobatics, multiple explosions and shoot outs, *Face/Off* required an enormous team of artists and technicians working around the clock months in advance of principal photography to achieve director John Woo's vision.

The film was shot primarily in practical locations, although a small portion was filmed on stages at the Paramount lot. A dramatic shoot out in a loft was filmed on the ninth and tenth floors of an empty building located in downtown Los Angeles. With circular windows that overlook the urban skyline of L. A., its massive scale and rooftop accessibility made it a unique location. 'The loft is extraordinary,' felt Reuther. 'It shows the offbeat glamour and allure of the underworld in which Castor lives and the dark side of his character in a space large enough for John Woo to stage the most spectacular gun fight.'

The entirety of the loft, including the walls and furniture, was rigged with over 5,000 bullet effects. Shooting entirely at night, director of photography Oliver Wood lit the sequence to highlight both the splendour of the setting and the movement taking place within it. It is here that Woo achieves another of his trademark cartoon action sequences, as the bad guys try to escape a raid by the FBI. Slow motion and balletic gun play are set to Olivia Newton John singing 'Over the Rainbow' from *The Wizard Of Oz*.

Nic once again made sure that stuntmen took most of the risks in the film – but that didn't stop him getting put in at least one awkward situation. A pivotal moment required him to be precariously balanced on the top of a privately-owned oil platform three miles off the coast of Carpenteria in the Pacific ocean, which was doubling as the high-tech prison in which Archer is trapped until he escapes. Nic, afraid of heights, described his feelings: 'I was on top of this 200-foot oil rig without much of a ledge. It was one of the more frightening days of my life.'

Shooting also took place at Southern California International Aviation, formerly known as George Airforce Base, where the actors and director had ample space to play out the death-defying chase of a Jet Star plane. The airport provided the crew with total control of a runway 10,000 feet long to film the dramatic action sequence which opens the film. Later, Archer and Castor's pursuit of one another took to the water in an unprecedented boat chase through the Port of Los Angeles in San Pedro. But despite brilliant action, designs and special effects the film belongs to the actors, according to producer Barrie Osborne. 'It's their performances that make this movie,' he said of the two stars. 'They are the ones that achieve the illusion of two characters switching places.'

'I assure you there are some weird, weird things in it,' Nic said of *Face/Off*. 'When I first signed on, it was because of Woo, who I think is a master *auteur*, and Travolta. But it wasn't until I started working on it that I began to see the potential to go pretty deep. There's a lot of bizarre behaviour there. When I become John's character, I become a man who is literally wearing the face of the man who shot his son.' Travolta joked that the pairing of him and Nicolas Cage was 'just like Joan Crawford and Bette Davis'.

Face/Off had a lot to do to top *The Rock* and *Con Air*, and it didn't quite pull it off, despite being a huge commercial success. Nevertheless, less than a month after *Con Air* had swept all before it at the box office, *Face/Off* did the same, opening on 29 June 1997. The film took $23.5 million over the opening weekend, beating Disney's *Hercules*'s $21.5 million and reaching over $110 million by September 1997. Now with three successive films each grossing over $100 million in a matter of months, Nic's asking price per film exceeded $7 million. But the money he was paid for each job was something he didn't like talking about – and, indeed, felt sensitive about, according to his friend, Jim Carrey. 'He's never really come out and said this, but I don't think he likes the idea that it's plastered everywhere what he's earning,' Carrey claimed. 'I don't think he wants it to overshadow the work itself. That people are thinking "money" when they see him. I don' t think that was ever his intention. I do think that he felt that if that cheque [his ambition to earn as much as Uncle Francis] that he wrote to himself came true, which it did, it would not just mean money; it would mean that he could work with the best in the business.'

The final film in Nicolas Cage's action movie trio secured his place at the top of the Hollywood tree. The film got great reviews, led by *Entertainment Weekly*, which noted that *Face/Off* featured 'the development of character with the smallest of gestures (Travolta's Archer runs his hand over the faces of those he loves, Cage's Troy stoops to tie his brother's shoelace). But it is the steady accretion of hundreds of small moments in this elegant, high-spirited, intensely satisfying production that, toted up, makes everything right about this desperately welcome thriller.' The subtleties in the performances also caught the attention of the *San Francisco Chronicle*. 'Travolta and Cage do more than switch roles. They switch styles. Travolta adopts Cage's abrupt gestures, crazy laugh and tilt of the head, while Cage amazingly embodies Travolta's soulfulness (as well as his tendency to stammer in emotional moments).' *USA Today* said, 'The best scenes in *Face/Off* are when things quiet down and Travolta and Cage get to explore the grim, uptight FBI agent and the lusty, vibrant terrorist (they both play both). It's a pleasure to watch them aping each other's mannerisms.'

'I'm done,' claimed Cage of his cinematic heroics. 'I like to really master a genre. After *Face/Off*, I will be done with action for a while. I feel like I've really done it. I've done every kind of genre of movie-making that I can imagine. I've done the underground art film, I've done dramatic movies, I've done comedies and now I've done action. I just want to have as many different careers within one career as I can possibly have and I hope to keep doing this to the end.'

11. Beautiful Freak

IT COMES AS A SURPRISE to many people when they realise that Nicolas Cage is only in his mid-thirties. He has almost always played parts older than his actual age, and his thinning pate and gangly build have played into that. 'I always looked older than my age,' he has lamented. Cage also admits to being annoyed when people think he always looks upset, claiming he can't help his hangdog expression. 'Sometimes people think I'm sad when I'm not. It's just the way I look.'

As the nineties approached their end, Nic had nothing at all to be sad about. He had his Oscar on the mantelpiece and he'd married the woman he always knew he would since the first day he'd met her, eight years before. He'd led the cast in three of the biggest blockbusters of the summers of 1996 and 1997. He was right at the top of the Hollywood A-list and had a full slate of mainstream film roles lined up before him.

In between movies, he was doing his best to ensure Patricia and he were not apart. In order that they could spend more time together he splashed out on a new holiday home in Malibu, which allowed them to escape from the madness and excess of Hollywood. The $3.6 million, five-bedroom 3,000 square foot home was located on an acre of land, right on the ocean, and boasted a cobblestone drive, a creek and a pool. The new home added to Nic's growing property portfolio, which now included his Hollywood Hills castle, a Victorian house in San Francisco and his Los Angeles apartment (which was now actually three apartments taking up the entire top floor of the building).

Not averse to spending his money, as he proudly boasted, Cage continued to splash out on cars. In March 1997 he'd spent almost half a million dollars to buy a 1971 Lamborghini Miura SVJ, last owned by the Shah of Iran. Bidding by phone to the sale in Geneva, Switzerland, Cage paid $446,820 – twice the actual value of the car, making it the most expensive car sold at auction in Europe during that year. The metallic-burgundy vehicle was one of only four SVJ's built and had been driven solely by the Shah's grandmother to and from church, clocking up a mere

1,897 miles in 25 years. After the revolution of 1979, the car had been seized by Islamic revolutionaries and locked away in a garage for being 'too decadent for government use'.

Cage had also achieved another ambition by having a letter published in *Playboy* magazine. While he thanked the publication for carrying out a courteous interview with him, he also castigated the editor for publishing unauthorised nude photos of actress Uma Thurman. She and Cage had been linked romantically in the past, but neither had confirmed or denied the details of any relationship. Nonetheless, Cage had risen to Thurman's defence, writing to the editor: 'Your pictorials have always been presented with quality and taste. As you stated in the layout, you are not fans of this type of photography, which leads me to wonder why the magazine chose to be so blatantly hypocritical.' *Playboy* responded by noting: 'When someone so celebrated and camera-worthy outs herself on display in public, it's disingenuous for her to be shocked that there were interested photographers in place.' No-one noted what Patricia Arquette thought of it all.

Coming out of *The Rock, Con Air* and *Face/Off*, Nicolas Cage had his choice of roles awaiting him. The first he started work on was *City Of Angels*, a reinvention of Wim Wenders' German film *Wings Of Desire* about an angel, played by Bruno Ganz, falling in love with a mere mortal. He began work on the film, in which he co-stars with Meg Ryan, in April 1997. The location of the action was switched from Berlin to Hollywood's own city of angels, Los Angeles. 'I quickly learned that to really play an angel is an almost impossible thing,' Nic said of the project. 'You can drive yourself nuts trying to interpret the whys and wherefores of the physics of angeldom. I don't blink, I don't have a shadow; it's very trippy. The best choice I could make was to find the most entertaining approach, without repeating what's been done of late. I want to maintain some sense of the concept that angels are terrifying, because they're not human. I don't want to be totally conversational and normal at it. I do want a sense of otherness, even if he is about love.'

Although lumbered with an entirely predictable plot, the combination of Nic and romantic comedy queen Meg Ryan in *City Of Angels* proved to be a huge box office hit. Released in April 1998 in the US, *City Of Angels* enjoyed a $15.3 million opening weekend and had grossed $63 million by the end of August 1998. The film took about £5 million when released in Britain. The weird edge brought to the film by the angelic crowds and the exuberant performance from Dennis Franz as fallen angel Mr Messinger brought *City Of Angels* a cult audience beyond the die-hard romantics.

According to *USA Today*, 'Cage tries to approximate Bruno Ganz's expertly somnambulent line readings. Unfortunately, the character comes off suggesting another of the black-comic nutcases Cage played early in his career', while Cage fan and *Chicago Sun-Times* film critic Roger Ebert thought the actor was 'more soppy and dewy-eyed than necessary'.

For Nic, playing the angelic Seth was a chance to get back to basics as far as

Nic teamed up with Meg Ryan for the romantic tale of an angel who wants to be human in City Of Angels.

his acting technique went. 'I'd been thinking a lot about my acting,' he said. 'I'd like to be able to get back to that place when I was a child, when I was awestruck by something that was as simple as a raindrop, or sunlight on my face. *City Of Angels* was a script that provided that for me, because I played a character who was in awe of people. In that awe I could convey my own feelings, as an actor, about the awe of being alive.'

Next on his agenda was Brian De Palma's thriller *Snake Eyes*, which had taken a while to get underway due to turmoil in the cast. Nic had signed up to play a detective who witnesses the assassination of the US Secretary of Defense during a boxing title fight, as a hurricane approaches Atlantic City. Nic had first been due to co-star with *Independence Day* star Will Smith for the *Mission: Impossible* director, but Smith soon dropped the film, leaving the way open for Al Pacino to take a role. Pacino – after months of prevarication – decided that the film wasn't for him either and Nic was without a co-star once again. As the delays mounted costs on the film soared, with De Palma getting $5 million to direct, writer David Koepp walking away with $4 million for the screenplay and Nic due to earn about $12 million. As the August 1997 shooting date drew closer, Paramount – the studio behind the film – finally signed up *Forest Gump* and *Ransom* star Gary Sinise to support Nic. Sinise's part was Kevin Dunne, a secret service agent who fails to protect the Secretary of Defense. Nic is his childhood friend, a local cop, who has to deal with the government conspiracy, track the killers and escape the

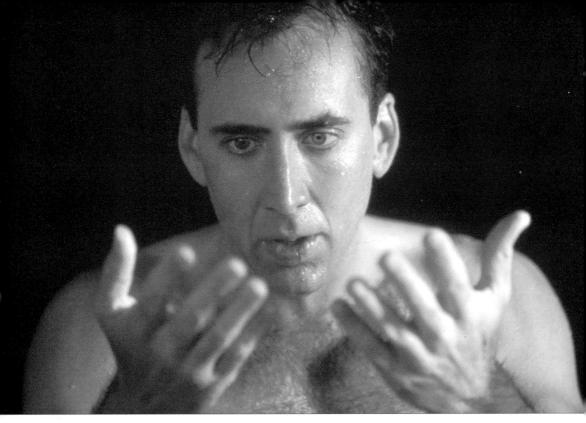

Awestruck by humanity, Seth (Nicolas Cage) gives up angelhood to be human for the love of Meg Ryan in City Of Angels.

hurricane. That proved to be no problem for the man who broke into *The Rock* and beat off the prisoners in *Con Air*.

For Nic, *Snake Eyes* was a return to the action adventure of *The Rock*, if not quite as over-the-top in scale and ambition. '*Snake Eyes* really is cinema,' he said. 'De Palma goes into *Rashomon* territory, into Akira Kurosawa's technique of showing everything about a story from other people's point-of-view. It's about an assassination, betrayal and who did it? It's a mystery-suspense-thriller with the accent on the suspense.'

After a battle between De Palma and the Motion Picture Association of America over what rating the film would be awarded, *Snake Eyes* opened on 9 August 1998, taking $16.3 million over the first weekend, climbing to $40.5 million by the end of that month.

The reviews were mixed, with the *Washington Post* picking out the film's good and bad points: 'As the cop Santoro, Cage is once again over the top but totally in control of his character, who swerves from moral confusion to blemished heroism. The sense of mystery in *Snake Eyes* evaporates all too quickly, as Santoro unravels the truth with the help of the arena's thousands of videos cameras – the technology that is used in much the same way in De Palma's more satisfying *Blow Out*. As film-making, it's a bravura performance, but as a film, it falls flat.' Todd McCarthy, writing in *Variety*, highlighted Cage's contribution: 'Cage supplies beaucoup energy, but his highly comprimised husler cop character provides little else in which he can invest his talent.'

The delays in getting started on *Snake Eyes* had caused new problems for Nic. In a bizarre casting twist he had been approached by Warner Brothers to take over the role of Superman, last played in films by the now crippled Christopher Reeve and, most recently, on TV by Dean Cain. No one seemed less like the traditional image of Superman than Nicolas Cage. Sure, he could probably do a great Clark Kent, but how could the balding, goofy guy from *Moonstruck, Peggy Sue Got Married* and *Raising Arizona* possibly play the superhuman Man of Steel? The casting controversy echoed Tim Burton's casting of comic actor Michael Keaton for the first *Batman* blockbuster in 1989. Some comic-book fans were outraged at the suggestion that the actor was suitable for the role. Nic, however, thought it would be great because his wife could claim she'd slept with Superman!

The new film, alternately titled *Superman Reborn* or *Superman Lives*, was to be drawn from some recent stories featured in the comic-book series, but scheduling conflicts with *Snake Eyes* looked likely to kill Nic's chance to don the famous red, white and blue outfit. Even Nicolas Cage couldn't be in two places at once, shooting two films simultaneously. Nic's agent, Richard Lovett at Creative Artists Agency, had set up the two deals, but now the twelve-week production schedule for *Snake Eyes* was to start on 1 August 1997, while *Superman* was set for an 6 October kick-off – creating a three-week overlap between the projects.

Neither studio was willing to change. Warner Brothers regarded the reinvention of *Superman* as a major franchise, and were making efforts to enlist the Burger King chain as promotional partners. Paramount wanted *Snake Eyes* to be a summer 1998 blockbuster in the style of *Face/Off*. Nic was vital to both studios – and it was up to him to decide. Eventually his agent informed Paramount that he would only participate in *Snake Eyes* if the dates could be shifted to make room for *Superman*. 'As much as Nic wanted to do *Snake Eyes*,' said a CAA executive, '*Superman* was more important.' Paramount claimed that Nic was contractually locked into their August start date, and complained that Lovett had been manipulating the situation.

As lawyers started to line up and Paramount prepared to sue CAA and Nic, the stand-off was resolved. Paramount offered to 'front load' Nic's scenes in *Snake Eyes* – that is, shoot all his scenes early in the production and they moved the start date forward by ten days. In return they got a unique commitment from Nic – if he had more work to do on *Snake Eyes* when it came time to put on the Superman costume, then he'd return after wrapping the latter picture to finish *Snake Eyes*. Relief broke out all round and Nic – who had been kept out of all the arguments and power broking by his agent – got down to work as the cop in a storm. 'I'm just glad it all worked out,' he said.

None of this resolved the controversy of casting him as Superman in the first place. Many couldn't imagine the image of Nic in Superman's tights, but it wasn't the first time he'd been asked to play a superhero. He'd briefly been considered for the film version of *The Incredible Hulk* and in December 1996 he had been offered the lead in *Iron Man*, a popular Marvel comic-book series about Tony Stark, a billionaire industrialist who dons the most advanced combat armour ever designed and aids those in distress. Nic had made clear his interest in comic-book roles in his *Playboy* interview, but he may have decided *Iron Man* was too close to the robotic superhero types he disliked – on the other hand, Superman was flesh and blood, albeit alien flesh and blood. That was what fascinated Cage about the role. 'I would make Superman a freak,' he said gleefully, aware of the impact of his words on the comic-book fans. 'He'd be a beautiful freak, in that he really cares about people. I wouldn't be afraid to talk about his loneliness and his feeling like an alien, never fitting in and so always compulsively needing to do heroic acts so people would like him and he would feel loved.'

In a further affront to comic-book fans, none other than Tim Burton was lined up by Warner Brothers to direct the new *Superman* epic. The production looked set to be a troubled one, though. Writer Kevin Smith, who'd made *Clerks* and *Chasing Amy*, and was a big comic-book and *Star Wars* fan was signed up by Warners to write the first draft of the screenplay. 'You'll never meet a more anxious bunch of motherfuckers in your life,' he said to *Buzz* magazine about the executives on the film. 'They're calling you every day: "What have you done for me lately? What's going on? When are we getting pages?" I'll think twice before signing on a studio film again.' Smith was removed from the project and set to work on his own film, *Dogma*.

Ironically, Nic did not don the mantle of Superman in October 1997 as had been scheduled, due to further delays in the production process. With a script still not ready and *Batman* scribe Wesley Strick brought on board by Tim Burton to start from scratch, the whole project was put back to begin shooting in April 1998. Although this delay caused Nic to rethink whether to stick with the film, he did see the role as the peak of his life to date as an actor. He was someone who had invented himself and selected his 'stage name' from that of his favourite comic-book character, the African-American superhero Luke Cage. Much of his career had been spent giving cartoon-like larger-than-life performances, even as an action hero. Now, he was hoping to play a superhero for real.

'I want to address the Superman character that hasn't really been examined before. Superman is an American myth. If I can play up Superman's feelings of being different or feeling weird, maybe I can get one little boy to stop teasing another little boy about being different. That's my thought process. Maybe it's a little weighty, but at least it's positive.' Nic had come full circle, back to the days when young Nicky Coppola had first played a part to fend off the school bullies who made his bus trip to school a misery. He still sympathised with the underdog.

Nic didn't regard *Superman* as somehow a 'lesser' project than some of his other films, claiming that comic-book characters were an important part of America's popular culture and this was his chance to play a modern mythic role. 'I'm trying to avoid being narrow-minded and pretentious, doing just what are regarded as important movies. Although I believe a movie like *Leaving Las Vegas* is important, I also believe that a movie like *Superman* has value. It all depends on your definition of what's important.' For Nic that included comic-book characters: 'The Greeks had their mythology and this is ours,' he said of *Superman*. 'Mickey

Snake Eyes saw Cage play a flawed and corrupt detective – but he's the only one who can solve the case.

Mouse and Batman and Superman and Coca- Cola – they're our pride. The story of Batman is a modern myth.'

Due to a lack of workable script and new questions about Nic's suitability for the role of Superman, the film was put on indefinite hold by Warner Brothers. Nic was upset and remained determined to bring his version of the Man of Steel to the big screen, even though Warner Brothers made strenuous efforts to switch his $20 million pay-or-play commitment to another of their upcoming films.

While waiting to wear the Superman outfit, Nic found himself with an unexpected opening in his schedule. Rather than relax, he made good use of the time, opting to take the leading role in *8 Millimeter*, a gritty, low-budget movie about the shady world of so-called 'snuff' films. The biggest surprise was that the script, by *Seven* writer Andrew Kevin Walker, was to be directed by *Batman And Robin* director Joel Schumacher.

Nic plays an investigator hired by a woman to uncover whether a snuff film she has found in her husband's vault is real. Co-starring is Joaquin Phoenix, younger brother of the late River Phoenix, who'd made an impact as the lovestruck killer in *To Die For*. He plays Nic's tour guide into the sleazy world of underground movies. '*8 Millimeter* is a very grim movie,' warned Cage before the film's late-Autumn 1998 release in the United States.

Following *8 Millimeter*, Nic had a number of projects to choose from. He'd made a commitment to star in Terry Gilliam's film *The Defective Detective* if the film ever came together. He'd been suggested, along with Tom Hanks and Edward Norton as a candidate to play Andy Kaufman in a biopic of the *Taxi* star who'd died of lung cancer in 1984 at the age of 36. Milos Forman was on board to direct, and Kaufman's *Taxi* co-star Danny De Vito was a driving force behind the project. One film that looked more certain was *Heartbreaker Inc.* to be made for Touchstone. Nic was set to play an adept seducer who's hired by lovelorn men to break the hearts of women who have rejected them. Of course, sparks fly when he falls in love with an assignment. It was a project which contained a personal interest for Nic – a chance to work out some of the anxieties remaining from his relationships with Christina Fulton and Kristen Zang.

Before any of these speculative projects could come to anything, Nic leapt at the chance to work with his wife Patricia Arquette on a film directed by Martin Scorsese. *Bring Out The Dead*, produced by Paramount and Touchstone, started production in New York in September 1998, and saw the married couple work together for the first time. Nic plays a burned-out paramedic who is haunted by the people he's sent to save – especially those he fails to save. After that film, it was possible that Nic would be taking the lead in Woody Allen's next film, after the Leonardo DiCaprio-starrer *Celebrity*. 'I can't talk about that,' is all Nic would tell *Esquire* about the intriguing possibility of a Cage–Allen combination.

As a way of broadening his influence on the films he made – and having claimed not to be interested in directing – Nic started work on a screenplay he hoped one day to produce, but his early efforts seemed doomed to failure. 'I had 70 pages of a script I was working on, which was in some ways autobiographical, about an actor who's on the run from dark forces. Well, it's not entirely autobiographical, but the guy is an actor. I think it's best when you write, to write about something you know.'

Before the project could get to a producer or director, the 'dark forces' Nic was writing about seemed to intervene to destroy his first attempt at a screenplay. He had been writing the script on his laptop computer, which he left outside his car one day upon leaving his house. 'I thought it was in the car,' he recalled, 'and I started the car, and I put the car in reverse, and ran over my briefcase and I smashed my computer.' He'd not made a backup copy and it seemed as if the accident had killed off his nascent screenwriting career. 'The technology tends to scare me now,' he claimed. 'It frightened me. I have not gotten back on a computer since.'

Whatever he did in the future, Nic was certain he wouldn't change too much. 'Shock is still fun,' he announced. 'I won't ever shut the door on it. There's not enough eccentricity in my life now. It's pretty much about family and work at the moment. But it's important to keep that eccentric spirit alive, because when that goes, I think the work will go. So, when I have a day to myself, I like to try to find ways of doing something unique with it. One of the things I like to do is go downtown – to Little Tokyo and Chinatown and Olvera Street – and pretend like I've gone to different parts of the world without ever having left L.A.'

Working in time to spend together became very important to both Nic and Patricia as their movie roles took them apart for long periods of time. 'It's rare to find somebody you can actually call your soulmate,' Nic said of his wife, 'but I do sense in her the same spirit that's in me, and I think she feels the same way. We identify with each other, and I've seen that in her work.' After *Bring Out The Dead*, the pair were keen to work together again and have given some thought to starring in an updated version of *The Thin Man*, playing the William Powell and Myrna Loy roles.

Nic set up his own production company during 1997 with his friend and frequent personal assistant Jeff Levine. Levine – also an actor – had featured in bit parts in several of Nic's films. According to Levine, they planned to use their company, called Saturn Films, to produce 'movies with morality, more passion and chivalry and a sense of what it means to be honourable'. As for Nic, he felt the need to return to a more 'old-fashioned' type of film: 'Movies like *High Noon* were once acceptable – that sort of code of honour that makes a man stop his wedding day and do the right thing.'

The first project lined up by Saturn Films was *Tom Slick: Monster Hunter*, a family movie in which Nic aimed to play the title role. In a deal with 20th Century Fox, the film was to be based on a treatment by Jib Polhemus. *Variety* noted the project, loosely based on a real-life adventurer from the fifties, was to be a comedy action escapade about an oil tycoon who spends his family fortune on a global quest to track down the world's legendary monsters, including the Yeti and the Loch Ness Monster. The real-life Slick was the subject of a 1989 book by Loren Coleman titled *Tom Slick And The Search For The Yeti*.

Nic also planned to produce and star in a remake of *The Courtship Of Eddie's Father*, the 1963 film starring Glenn Ford and a very young Ron Howard, now a film director (*Apollo 13*) himself. Ford played a widower who struggles to find a new wife who meets the approval of his young son (Howard). The film was also the basis for an ABC TV series starring Bill Bixby and Brandon Cruz that ran from 1969–72.

Nic was said to be interested in the project because his own son, Weston, was approximately the age of the young boy in the original picture. Although no one else was attached to the Warner Brothers project, it was made clear that Ron Howard wouldn't be working on the remake. Nic was also considering a film to be called *Family Man* for a possible shoot in early 1999.

Nicolas Cage had started his screen life early, and by the time of his major success in his mid-thirties he was producing his best work. 'I started acting when I was 16 and I had to learn, and fall on my face, and grow up, publicly, through trial and error,' he noted. 'I'm still having to make excuses for films I made when I was sixteen. Now, I've gotten to the point where I feel like the camera is my friend. I'm excited by it when I see it, it's like flirting with it. It's like pursuing a woman, sometimes. If you chase too hard, it runs away. If you ignore it, it comes to you. Sometimes the only time an actor does relax is when he's on camera.'

Secure in his position in Hollywood after his Best Actor Oscar win, Nicolas Cage was happy to look back over his career, grateful for all that acting had given him and even saved him from. 'Acting for me is this incredibly sacred hero that

NICOLAS CAGE – HOLLYWOOD'S WILD TALENT

came in and saved my life,' he admitted. 'To me, it's been like a therapy – it's what kept me balanced, kept me with a sense of purpose. I could get all the stuff out of me that I had, all that fire – anger, or love or lust. Anything.'

While crediting his acting career with having saved him from some of his demons, Nic is equally happy to claim that the source of his often astonishing onscreen performances comes from something warped within himself. 'I fear in some ways losing balance,' he said, harking back to his mother's bouts of insanity during his childhood. 'I know that my ideas and feelings are applicable to the nature of the work that I do. I'd rather they go somewhere productive than explode on myself; in other words, it seems that I'm avoiding some kind of insanity. That's why I work so hard.'

Whatever he was to tackle next, it was sure to be unique, startling and different. Nic had set out on his career as an actor with an ambition. He'd wanted to emulate the success and wealth of his Uncle Francis. If Francis Ford Coppola had been the driving force of his career, the actor had surpassed any measures of success which could be applied. None of that, though, had solved any of the family problems of the Coppola clan. The tensions between Francis and Nic's father August had never really been resolved, and Nic's relationship with his father had gone from bad to worse.

When Nic's choice to become an actor and change his name was validated by the Best Actor Oscar, both Francis and August had to acknowledge the choices Nicolas had made. 'Francis sent me a basket of flowers when I won the Oscar,' Nic said, 'and I got a congratulatory telegram from my father. We're okay. You can take this as you want, but I try not to let that competitive side of myself come into play. It does go back hundreds of years, though, to the old country.'

A reconciliation – even a frosty one – that Nic claimed had happened in his family would not lead him to change his name back to Coppola, though. It was far too late – he had become the character he'd created back when he started out acting. 'I've become who I am now and that's Nicolas Cage. Nicolas Coppola is not around any more.'

Filmography

The Best of Times
USA 1981 TV Movie 95 minutes
Cast: Nicolas Cage, Jill Schoelen

Fast Times At Ridgemont High
USA 1982, 92 minutes
Directed by Amy Heckerling
Screenplay by Cameron Crowe, based on his novel
Production Company: Universal Pictures
Cast: Sean Penn (Jeff Spicoli), Jennifer Jason Leigh
(Stacy Hamilton), Judge Reinhold (Brad Hamilton),
Robert Romanus (Mike Damone), Brian Backer
(Mark 'Rat' Ratner), Phoebe Cates (Linda Barrett),
Ray Walston (Mr Hand), Scott Thomson (Arnold),
Vincent Schiavelli (Mr. Vargas), Amanda Wyss (Lisa),
D. W. Brown (Ron Johnson), Forest Whitaker
(Charles Jefferson), Kelli Maroney (Cindy), Tom
Nolan (Dennis Taylor), Blair Ashleigh (Pat Bernardo),
Eric Stoltz (Bud), Stanley Davis Jr (Jefferson's
Brother), James Russo (Robber), Nicolas Coppola
[Cage] (Brad's Buddy), Reginald Farmer (Vice
Principal), Anthony Edwards (Stoner)

Rumble Fish
USA 1983, 94 minutes
Directed by Francis Ford Coppola
Screenplay by Francis Ford Coppola and S. E.
Hinton, based on his novel
Production Company: Zoetrope Studios/Universal
Cast: Matt Dillon (Rusty James), Mickey Rourke (The
Motorcycle Boy), Diane Lane (Patty), Dennis Hopper
(Father), Diana Scarwid (Cassandra), Vincent Spano
(Steve), Nicolas Cage (Smokey), Chris Penn (B.J.
Jackson), Laurence Fishburne (Midget), Gian-Carlo
Coppola (Cousin James), Sofia Coppola (Patty's
sister), S. E. Hinton (Hooker)

Valley Girl (Bad Boyz)
USA 1983, 95 minutes
Directed by Martha Coolidge
Screenplay by Wayne Crawford and Andrew Lane
Production Company: Valley 9000 / Atlantic
Releasing Corp
Cast: Nicolas Cage (Randy), Deborah Foreman
(Julie), Elizabeth Daily (Loryn), Michael Bowen
(Tommy), Cameron Dye (Fred), Heidi Holicker
(Stacey), Michelle Meyrink (Suzie), Tina Theberge
(Samantha), Lee Purcell (Beth), Frederic Forrest
(Steve Richman)

Racing With The Moon
USA 1984, 108 minutes
Directed by Richard Benjamin
Screenplay by Steven Kloves
Production Company: Paramount Pictures
Cast: Sean Penn (Henry 'Hopper' Nash), Elizabeth
McGovern (Caddie Winger), Nicolas Cage (Nicky),
John Karlen (Mr Nash), Rutanya Alda (Mrs Nash),
Max Showalter (Mr Arthur), Crispin Glover (Gatsby

Boy), Barbara Howard (Gatsby Girl), Bob Maroff
(Al), Dominic Nardini (Soldier with Annie), John
Brandon (Mr Kaiser), Eve Brent Ashe (Mrs Kaiser),
Suzanne Adkinson (Sally), Shawn Schepps
(Gretchen), Charles Miller (Arnie), Patricia Allison
(Mrs Spangler), Michael Madsen (Frank), Dana
Carvey (Baby Face), Carol Kane (Annie)

The Cotton Club
USA 1984, 127 minutes
Directed by Francis Ford Coppola
Screenplay by William Kennedy and Francis
Coppola, based upon a story by William Kennedy,
and Francis Coppola and Mario Puzo
Production Company: Zoetrope Studios / Orion
Cast: Richard Gere (Dixie Dwyer), Gregory Hines
(Sandman Williams), Diane Lane (Vera Cicero),
Lonette McKee (Lea Rose Oliver), Bob Hoskins
(Owney Madden), James Remar (Dutch Schultz),
Nicolas Cage (Vincent Dwyer), Allen Garfield
(Abbadabba Berman), Fred Gwynne (Frenchy
Demange), Gwen Verdon (Tish Dwyer), Lisa Jane
Persky (Frances Flegenheimer), Maurice Hines (Clay
Williams), Julian Beck (Sol Weinstein), Novella
Nelson (Madame St. Clair), Laurence Fishburne
(Bumpy Rhodes), John P. Ryan (Joe Flynn), Tom
Waits (Irving Stark), Jennifer Grey (Patsy Dwyer), Joe
Dallesandro (Charles 'Lucky' Luciano), Diane Venora
(Gloria Swanson), Tucker Smallwood (Kid Griffin),
Woody Strode (Holmes), James Russo (Vince Hood),
Giancarlo Esposito (Bumpy Hood), Marc Coppola
(Ted Husing), Sofia Coppola (Child in Street)

Birdy
USA 1984, 120 minutes
Directed by Alan Parker
Screenplay by Jack Behr and Sandy Kroopf, based on
the novel by William Wharton
Production Company: TriStar / A&M Films
Cast: Matthew Modine (Birdy), Nicolas Cage (Al
Columbato), John Harkins (Doctor Weiss), Sandy
Baron (Mr. Columbato), Karen Young (Hannah
Rourke), Bruno Kirby (Renaldi), Nancy Fish (Mrs
Prevost), George 'Buck' Flower (Birdy's father),
Dolores Sage (Birdy's mother), Robert L. Ryan (Joe
Sagessa), James Santini (Mario Columbato)

The Boy In Blue
Canada 1984/1986, 100 minutes
Directed by Charles Jarrott
Screenplay by Douglas Bowie
Production Company: Canadian Broadcasting
Corporation (CBC) / Regatta Productions / Téléfilm
Canada
Cast: Nicolas Cage (Ned Hanlan), Cynthia Dale
(Margaret), Christopher Plummer (Knox), David
Naughton (Bill), Sean Sullivan (Walter), Melody
Anderson (Dulcie), James B. Douglas (Collins),
Walter Massey (Mayor), Austin Willis (Bainbridge),
Philip Craig (Kinnear), Robert McCormick (Trickett)

Peggy Sue Got Married
USA 1986, 104 minutes

157

Directed by Francis Ford Coppola
Screenplay by Jerry Leichtling and Arlene Sarner
Production Company: TriStar
Cast: Kathleen Turner (Peggy Sue), Nicolas Cage
(Charlie Bodell), Barry Miller (Richard Norvik),
Catherine Hicks (Carol Heath), Joan Allen (Maddy
Nagle), Kevin J. O'Connor (Michael Fitzsimmons),
Jim Carrey (Walter Getz), Lisa Jane Persky (Delores
Dodge), Lucinda Jenney (Rosalie Testa), Wil Shriner
(Arthur Nagle), Barbara Harris (Evelyn Kelcher),
Don Murray (Jack Kelcher), Sofia Coppola (Nancy
Kelcher), Maureen O'Sullivan (Elizabeth Alvorg)

Raising Arizona
USA 1987, 94 minutes
Directed by Joel Coen
Screenplay by Ethan Coen and Joel Coen
Production Company: Circle Films
Cast: Nicolas Cage (H. I. McDonnough), Holly
Hunter (Ed), Trey Wilson (Nathan Arizona Sr.), John
Goodman (Gale), William Forsythe (Evelle), Sam
McMurray (Glen), Frances McDormand (Dot),
Randall 'Tex' Cobb (Leonard Smalls), T.J. Kuhn
(Nathan Junior), Lynne Dumin Kitei (Florence
Arizona), Peter Benedek (Prison Counsellor), M.
Emmet Walsh (Machine Shop Ear-Bender)

Moonstruck
USA 1987, 102 minutes
Directed by Norman Jewison
Screenplay by John Patrick Shanley
Production Company: MGM (Metro-Goldwyn-
Mayer) [aka MGM-UA]
Cast: Cher (Loretta Castorini), Nicolas Cage (Ronny
Cammareri), Vincent Gardenia (Cosmo Castorini),
Olympia Dukakis (Rose Castorini), Danny Aiello
(Johnny Cammareri), Julie Bovasso (Rita
Cappomaggi), John Mahoney (Perry), Louis Guss
(Raymond Cappomaggi), Feodor Chaliapin Jr. (Old
Man), Anita Gillette (Mona), Nada Despotovich
(Chrissy), Catherine Scorsese (Customer at Bakery)

Never On Tuesday
USA 1988 90 minutes
Directed by Adam Rifkin
Screenplay by Adam Rifkin
Production Company: Palisades Entertainment Corp.
Cast: Claudia Christian (Tuesday), Andrew Lauer
(Matt), Peter Berg (Eddie), Dave Anderson, Mark
Garbarino, Melvyn Pearls, Brett Seals (Zombies).
Uncredited cast: Nicolas Cage (Man in Red Sports
Car), Cary Elwes (Tow Truck Driver), Emilio Estevez
(Tow Truck Driver), Gilbert Gottfried (Lucky Larry
Lupin), Judd Nelson (Cop), Charlie Sheen (Thief)

Vampire's Kiss
USA 1989, 96 minutes
Directed by Robert Bierman
Screenplay by Joseph Minion
Production Company: Magellan Pictures
Cast: Nicolas Cage (Peter Loew), Maria Conchita
Alonso (Alva Restrepo), Jennifer Beals (Rachel),
Elizabeth Ashley (Dr Glaser), Kasi Lemmons (Jackie),

Bob Lujan (Emilio), Jessica Lundy (Sharon), John
Walker (Donald), Boris Leskin (Fantasy Cabbie),
Michael Knowles (Andrew), John Michael Higgins
(Ed), Jodie Markell (Joke Girl), Marc Coppola (Joke
Guy), David Hyde Pierce (Theater Guy)

Fire Birds (Wings Of The Apache)
USA 1990, 85 minutes
Directed by David Green
Screenplay by Paul F. Edwards and Nick Thiel, based on
a story by Dale Dye, John K. Swensson and Step Tyner
Production Company: Nova International Films
Cast: Nicolas Cage (Jake Preston), Tommy Lee Jones
(Brad Little), Sean Young (Billie Lee Guthrie), Bryan
Kestner (Breaker), Dale Dye (A.K. McNeil), Mary
Ellen Trainor (Janet Little), J. A. Preston (General
Olcott), Peter Onorati (Rice), Charles Lanyer (Darren
Phillips), Illana Shoshan (Sharon Geller), Marshall R.
Teague (Doug Daniels)

Wild At Heart
USA 1990 124 minutes
Directed by David Lynch
Screenplay by David Lynch, based on the novel by
Barrie Gifford
Production Company: PolyGram Filmed
Entertainment / Propaganda Films
Cast: Nicolas Cage (Sailor Ripley), Laura Dern
(Lula), Willem Dafoe (Bobby Peru), J. E. Freeman
(Santos), Crispin Glover (Dell), Diane Ladd (Marietta
Fortune / Wicked Witch), Calvin Lockhart (Reggie),
Isabella Rossellini (Perdita), Harry Dean Stanton
(Johnnie Farragut), Grace Zabriskie (Juana), Sherilyn
Fenn (Girl in accident), Marvin Kaplan (Uncle
Pooch), William Morgan Sheppard (Mr. Reindeer),
David Patrick Kelly (Dropshadow), Freddie Jones
(George Kovich), John Lurie (Sparky), Jack Nance
(Spool), Pruitt Taylor Vince (Buddy), Sheryl Lee
(Glinda, the Good Witch)

Industrial Symphony No. 1: The Dream Of The
Broken Hearted
USA 1990, TV Movie 50 minutes
Directed by David Lynch
Screenplay / Music by Angelo Badalamenti and
David Lynch
Production Company: Frost / Lynch Productions
Cast: Michael J. Anderson (Little Man), Nicolas Cage
(Heartbreaking Man), Julee Cruise (The Dreamself of
the Heartbroken Woman), Laura Dern (Heartbroken
Woman)

Zandalee
USA 1990, 100 minutes
Directed by Sam Pillsbury
Screenplay by Mari Kornhauser
Production Company: Electric Pictures
Cast: Nicolas Cage (Johnny), Judge Reinhold
(Thierry), Erika Anderson (Zandalee), Joe Pantoliano
(Gerri), Viveca Lindfors (Talla), Aaron Neville (Jack),
Steve Buscemi (OPP Man), Ian Abercrombie (Louis
Medina), Marisa Tomei (Remy), Jo-El Sonnier
(Bartender), Newell Alexander (Allen Calhoun),

Tempo di uccidere (Time to Kill / The Short Cut)
Italy 1990, 90 minutes
Directed by Giuliano Montaldo
Screenplay by Giuliano Montaldo, based on the
novel by Ennio Flaiano
Cast: Nicolas Cage, Ricky Tognazzi, Patrice Flora
Praxo, Gianluca Favilla, Georges Claisse, Robert
Liensol, Vittorio Amendola, Mario Mazzarotto,
Michele Melega, Franco Trevisi, Giancarlo Giannini

Honeymoon In Vegas
USA 1992, 92 minutes
Directed by Andrew Bergman
Screenplay by Andrew Bergman
Production Company: New Line Cinema
Cast: James Caan (Tommy Korman), Nicolas Cage
(Jack Singer), Sarah Jessica Parker (Betsy / Flashback
Donna), Pat Morita (Mahi Mahi), Johnny Williams
(Johnny Sandwich), John Capodice (Sally Molars),
Robert Costanzo (Sidney Tomashefsky), Anne
Bancroft (Bea Singer), Peter Boyle (Chief Orman)

Amos And Andrew
USA 1993, 95 minutes
Directed by E. Max Frye
Screenplay by E. Max Frye
Production Company: Castle Rock
Entertainment / New Line Cinema
Cast: Nicolas Cage (Amos Odell), Samuel L. Jackson
(Andrew Sterling), Michael Lerner (Phil Gillman),
Margaret Colin (Judy Gillman), Dabney Coleman
(Chief Tolliver), Brad Dourif (Officer Donaldson),
Giancarlo Esposito (Rev. Brunch), Bob Balaban
(Doctor Fink), Tracey Walter (Bloodhound Bob)

Deadfall
USA 1993, 99 minutes
Directed by Christopher Coppola
Screenplay by Christopher Coppola, David Webb
Peoples and Nick Vallelonga
Production Company: Trimark Pictures
Cast: Michael Biehn (Joe), Sarah Trigger (Diane),
Nicolas Cage (Eddie), James Coburn (Mike / Lou),
Peter Fonda (Pete), Charlie Sheen (Morgan Gripp),
Talia Shire (Sam), J. Kenneth Campbell (Huey),
Michael Constantine (Frank), Marc Coppola (Bob),
Mickey Dolenz (Bart), Brian Donovan (Mitch), Renée
Estevez (Baby's Babe)

Red Rock West
USA 1992, 98 minutes
Directed by John Dahl
Screenplay by John Dahl and Rick Dahl
Production Company: Propaganda Films / Red Rock
Films
Cast: Nicolas Cage (Michael), Craig Reay (Jim),
Vance Johnson (Mr Johnson), Robert Apel (Howard),
Bobby Joe McFadden (Old Man), J. T. Walsh (Wayne),
Lara Flynn Boyle (Suzanne), Dennis Hopper (Lyle),
Dale Gibson (Kurt), Ted Parks (Cashier), Babs Bram
(Receptionist), Robert Guajardo (Doctor), Sarah
Sullivan (Nurse), Jeff Levine (Country Girl

Bartender)

Guarding Tess
USA 1995, 95 minutes
Directed by Hugh Wilson
Screenplay by Peter Torokvei and Hugh Wilson
Production Company: TriStar
Cast: Shirley MacLaine (Tess Carlisle), Nicolas Cage
(Doug Chesnic), Austin Pendleton (Earl Fowler),
Edward Albert (Barry Carlisle), James Rebhorn
(Howard Schaeffer), Richard Griffiths (Frederick),
John Roselius (Tom Bahlor), Hugh Wilson (Voice of
the President), David Graf (Lee Danielson), Don
Yesso (Ralph Buoncristiani), James Lally (Joe
Spector), Dale Dye (Charles Ivy)

It Could Happen To You
USA 1994, 101 minutes
Directed by Andrew Bergman
Screenplay by Jane Anderson
Production Company: TriStar
Cast: Nicolas Cage (Charlie Lang), Bridget Fonda
(Yvonne Biasi), Rosie Perez (Muriel Lang), Wendell
Pierce (Bo Williams), Isaac Hayes (Angel), Victor
Rojas (Jesu), Seymour Cassel (Jack Gross), Stanley
Tucci (Eddie Biasi), J. E. Freeman (Sal Bontempo),
Red Buttons (Walter Zakuto)

Trapped In Paradise
USA 1994, 111 minutes
Directed by George Gallo
Screenplay by George Gallo
Production Company: 20th Century Fox
Cast: Nicolas Cage (Bill Firpo), Richard B. Shull
(Father Ritter), Jon Lovitz (Dave Firpo), Mädchen
Amick (Sarah Collins), Dana Carvey (Alvin Firpo),
Jack Heller (Chief Parole Officer), Mike Steiner
(Monty Dealer), Florence Stanley (Ma Firpo), Jeff
Levine (Man in Restaurant)

A Century Of Cinema
USA 1994, Documentary, 72 minutes
Directed by Caroline Thomas
Screenplay by Bob Thomas
Featured a host of film stars and directors, including
Nicolas Cage, discussing 100 years of cinema

Kiss Of Death
USA 1995, 102 minutes
Directed by Barbet Schroeder
Screenplay by Richard Price, based on the 1947
screenplay by Ben Hecht and Charles Lederer from a
story by Eleazar Lipsky
Production Company: 20th Century Fox
Cast: David Caruso (Jimmy Kilmartin), Samuel L.
Jackson (Calvin), Nicolas Cage (Little Junior Brown),
Helen Hunt (Bev Kilmartin), Kathryn Erbe (Rosie
Kilmartin), Stanley Tucci (Frank Zioli), Michael
Rapaport (Ronnie), Ving Rhames (Omar), Philip
Baker Hall (Big Junior Brown), Anthony Heald (Jack
Gold), Angel David (J. J.), Richard Price (City Clerk)
Leaving Las Vegas
USA 1995, 111 minutes

Directed by Mike Figgis
Screenplay by Mike Figgis, based on the novel by
John O' Brien
Production Company: Initial Productions / Lumière
Pictures
Cast: Nicolas Cage (Ben), Elisabeth Shue (Sera),
Julian Sands (Yuri), Richard Lewis (Peter), Steven
Weber (Marc Nussbaum), Valeria Golino (Terri),
Vincent Ward (Businessman), Lucinda Jenney (Weird
Woman), French Stewart (Businessman), Ed Lauter
(Mobster), Waldemar Kalinowski (Mobster), Mike
Figgis (Mobster), R. Lee Ermey (Conventioneer),
Danny Huston (Barman), Laurie Metcalf (Landlady),
Shawnee Smith (Biker Girl), Julian Lennon
(Bartender at biker bar), Bob Rafelson (Man at mall),
Marc Coppola (Dealer)

The Rock
USA 1996, 135 minutes
Directed by Michael Bay
Screenplay by David Weisberg and Douglas S. Cook
and Mark Rosner, based on a story by David
Weisberg and Douglas S. Cook
Production Company: Don Simpson / Jerry
Bruckheimer Films / Hollywood Pictures
Cast: Sean Connery (John Patrick Mason), Nicolas
Cage (Stanley Goodspeed), Ed Harris (General
Francis X. Hummel), John Spencer (FBI Director
Womack), David Morse (Major Tom Baxter), William
Forsythe (Paxton), Michael Biehn (Commander
Anderson), Vanessa Marcil (Carla Pestalozzi), John
C. McGinley (Marine Captain Hendrix), Gregory
Sporleder (Captain Frye), Tony Todd (Captain
Darrow), Bokeem Woodbine (Sergeant Crisp), Jim
Maniaci (Private Scarpetti), Greg Collins (Private
Gamble), Marshall R. Teague (Seal Reigert)

Con Air
USA 1997, 115 minutes
Directed by Simon West
Screenplay by Scott Rosenberg
Production Company: Jerry Bruckheimer Pictures /
Buena Vista Pictures / Touchstone Pictures
Cast: Nicolas Cage (Cameron Poe), John Cusack (US
Marshal Vince Larkin), John Malkovich (Cyrus 'The
Virus' Grissom), Steve Buscemi (Garland 'The
Marietta Mangler' Greene), Ving Rhames (Nathan
'Diamond Dog' Jones), Colm Meaney (Agent Duncan
Malloy), Mykelti Williamson ('Baby O' O'dell),
Rachel Ticotin (Sarah Bishop), Monica Potter (Tricia
Poe), David Chappelle (Pinball), M.C. Gainey (Jimmy
Earl 'Swamp Thing' West, John Roselius (Devers),
Renoly Santiago (Sally-Can't Dance), Danny Trejo
(John 'Johnny 23' Baca), Doug Hutchinson (Donald)

Face / Off
USA 1997, 138 minutes
Directed by John Woo
Screenplay by Mike Werb and Michael Colleary
Production Company: WCG Entertainment
Productions / Douglas / Reuther Productions /
Paramount Pictures / Touchstone Pictures
Cast: John Travolta (Sean Archer), Nicolas Cage
(Castor Troy), Joan Allen (Eve Archer), Alessandro
Nivola (Pollux Troy), Gina Gershon (Sasha Hassler),

Dominique Swain (Jamie Archer), Nick Cassavetes
(Dietrich Hassler), Harve Presnell (Lazzaro), Colm
Feore (Dr Malcolm Walsh), John Carroll Lynch
(Prison Guard Walton), CCH Pounder (Hollis Miller),
Robert Wisdom (Tito), Margaret Cho (Wanda), Jamie
Denton (Buzz), Matt Ross (Loomis), Dana Smith
(Lars)

City of Angels
USA 1998, 117 minutes
Directed by Brad Silberling
Screenplay by Dana Stevens and Wim Wenders,
based on the screenplay Wings Of Desire / Himmel
über Berlin, Der (1987) by Wim Wenders
Production Company: Atlas Entertainment
Cast: Nicolas Cage (Seth), Meg Ryan (Maggie Rice),
André Braugher (Cassiel), Dennis Franz (Messinger)

Snake Eyes
USA 1998, 107 minutes
Directed by Brian DePalma
Screenplay by David Koepp
Production Company: Paramount Pictures
Cast: Nicolas Cage (Detective Rick Santoro), Carla
Gugino (Julia Costello), John Heard (Mr Powell),
Stan Shaw (Lincoln Tyler), Gary Sinise (Major Kevin
Dunne)

Works in Progress:

8MM (Eight Millimetre)
USA 1998
Directed by Joel Shumacher
Screenplay by Andrew Kevin Walker
Production Company: Columbia
Cast: Nicolas Cage (Tom Welles), Joaquin Phoenix
(Max)

Free Money
Canada 1998
Directed by Yves Simoneau
Production Company: Filmline International
(Enemy) Inc.
Cast: Alec Baldwin, Marlon Brando, Nicolas Cage,
Thomas Haden Church, John Cusack, Seiko
Matsuda, Charlie Sheen, Alicia Silverstone, Mira
Sorvino, Donald Sutherland

Bring Out the Dead
USA 1999
Directed by Martin Scorsese
Production Company: Paramount / Touchstone
Cast: Nicolas Cage, Patricia Arquette

Tom Slick – Monster Hunter (working title)
USA 1999
Production Company: Saturn Films
Cast: Nicolas Cage

The Courtship of Eddie's Father
USA 1999
Production Company: Saturn Films
Cast: Nicolas Cage